D0507500

500 Digital Video

Hints, Tips, and Techniques

RotoVision

A RotoVision Book
Published and distributed by RotoVision SA
Route Suisse 9, CH-1295 Mies
Switzerland

RotoVision SA, Sales & Editorial Office
Sheridan House, 114 Western Road
Hove BN3 1DD, UK

Tel: +44 (0)1273 72 72 68
Fax: +44 (0)1273 72 72 69
Email: sales@rotovision.com
Web: www.rotovision.com

Copyright © RotoVision SA 2006

All rights reserved. No part of this publication
may be reproduced, stored in a retrieval system
or transmitted in any form or by any means,
electronic, mechanical, photocopying, recording
or otherwise, without permission of the
copyright holder.

10 9 8 7 6 5 4 3 2 1

ISBN: 2-940361-18-5

Designed by Studio Ink

Reprographics in Singapore by ProVision (Pte) Ltd.
Tel: +65 6334 7720
Fax: +65 6334 7721

Printed in Singapore by Star Standard Industries (Pte) Ltd.

500
Digital Video
Hints, Tips, and Techniques

The Easy, All-in-One Guide to those Inside
Secrets for Shooting Better Digital Video

Rob Hull and Jamie Ewbank

Contents

Video Capture

Video Editing

Video Output

Introduction

Reasons for Videomaking

Whether it's the most typical of family occasions, or the chance to capture a once-in-a-lifetime moment, there is always an impulse that makes us hit the record button on a camcorder. The list of reasons for videomaking is as boundless as your imagination, and as wide as your dreams!

For most videomakers, a camcorder provides the opportunity to make a record of something precious, and that can mean birthdays, parties, weddings, or vacations. But videomaking in the 21st century offers us all much more than just a collection of images. It's not simply a case of recording on your camcorder, and then trying to put on a videotape for others to see. Now there is a diverse number of ways for your family, your friends, and even unsuspecting members of the general public to see what you've done.

Computers, software packages, disk burners, and the Internet pave the way to sharing your precious, funny, dramatic, and poignant home videos. There is a wide selection of easy-to-use and affordable software to edit out the moments you don't want in your videos, and to then burn a movie onto a disk (CD or DVD). You can even put your movies on the Internet, or send them via email.

But let's return to that first emotion—to press the big record button and set up the chain of events that leads the way to becoming a videomaker...

You can, of course, record anything you point the camcorder at. But there are certain subjects that crop up time and time again. So, let's look at them.

Family occasions are the most common times for a camcorder to appear. The time we spend with our nearest and dearest is a great opportunity to record, and also gives you a wide group of people who'll want to see what you've done. Birthdays, vacations, weddings, engagement parties, anniversaries, reunions—they're all great times to document.

Vacations can make for exceptionally good material. Here you can record memories of an amazing location, or a first trip abroad with kids. You get the benefit of scenery that's different from "home," and you also get to see your family and friends in more relaxed moments—well you'd hope so, but if not that can make for great footage too!

Sport is also another superb shooting opportunity. From school sports events (with the school's permission), to your local football team, or even to improving your own tennis serve or golf swing, videomaking can be there to help.

Music and theater provide situations where you can often dictate how and what to record, as well as occasionally offering you the chance to shout "Stop!," and ask for a scene or song to be replayed.

While not often viewed as "hip," documentaries are wonderful for their sense of liberation. You can choose the subject and then see what happens, and because documentaries might be shot on-the-hoof, no one's going to be looking for great lighting or dazzling camerawork. No, what they want here is for you to get your story across.

And for those of you who do want to get creative and out-do the filmmaking greats, then there are all manner of stories to be told...

Ultimately, videomaking is about sharing images and sounds, and whatever way you go about it you should enjoy it, savor it, and squeeze every last moment of enjoyment out of it. Moments can be fleeting, and unless you're ready, you'll miss out. And no one wants that.

Camera types and formats

When it comes to recording your digital images, you have several formats that you can choose from. Each offers specific benefits, as well as perhaps having the odd disadvantage.

What will help you pick the right format? Well, think about where you want your video to end up, who will want to watch it, and what they will watch it on. There's no point sending a relative a Mini DV tape of your family vacation if they can't play it.

You should also consider your own home-viewing equipment. What computer do you have? Do you have a DVD player or are you using VHS? What if you want to upgrade your TV and computer, and add a home cinema setup to your system?

Never fear though, there is always a way around a problem. For example, you could transfer your Mini DV tape to a computer and then pick from a variety of disks to record onto. Your relatives could then play the disk on their DVD player or computer. Always remember that every camcorder, no matter what format, comes with cables to hook it up to a TV, so you can watch your footage direct from the recording device.

Digital8

With Digital8 a digital signal is recorded onto analog tape. You end up with a large camcorder, similar in size to bulky analog camcorders, but the image and sound quality is much better. Only Sony makes Digital8 camcorders.

Mini DV

This format uses digital tape to record your home movies.
The image and sound quality is usually excellent, and the
camcorders themselves can be very small. The camcorders
have many connections for TVs and computers, so they
are very versatile.

MICROMV

Another format that only Sony uses. MICROMV uses MPEG2 recording, just like DVD and Microdrive camcorders, but still records to tape. Some camcorders in the range can be used to access the Internet, and to send and receive emails. In terms of quality–not bad, but the camcorders can be very expensive.

DVD

Record your videos on disk. DVD recording uses a compression technology called MPEG2 to get the images onto a disk that's just three inches (8cm). This means they're smaller than the DVDs you put in your home player, but they can still be put in and played on them. Image and sound quality is generally very good, though sometimes rapid movement can lead to less than smooth video.

HARD DISK

Here, footage is recorded onto a hard disk (like that
on a computer or iPod). The hard disk can either be one
that's removed from the camcorder and put into another
device to transfer the footage, or it can be fixed in place
and footage will be transferred via a connection on
the camcorder.

REMOVABLE STORAGE

Similar in principle to hard disk storage, except this
time your camcorder stores its video and stills onto a
removable media card. The card (SD and Memory Stick
are two popular types) can be removed from, or inserted
into, the camcorder at any time. You can buy cards with
larger or smaller capacities depending on how long you
want to record for.

Images can still be transferred to a computer or shown
on a TV direct from the camcorder, or you can take out
the card and put it into a card reader that's connected to
your computer.

Image quality takes a back seat to convenience on many
of these types of camcorder, as the cams can be very,
very compact.

High Definition (HD) video recording offers users the very best in image quality. The camcorders are more expensive than other formats and are primarily aimed at semi-professional and professional users.

Images are recorded to tape but you will need to have a HD editing program to work with the footage on a computer, and an HD TV to view it.

Video on your cellphone

Many Smartphones and 3G phones allow you to shoot and edit sophisticated videos without having to invest in a video camera. Here are some hints and tips for the mobile videomaker.

The latest Smartphones and 3G mobiles allow you to shoot and edit video clips, and even add titles and special effects. With some phones you now have the option—with larger capacity SD and MMC cards—to boost the storage capacity and record an hour of video.

Unlike still images, video clips don't make use of your phone's megapixel quality. Instead, because the amount of space that video and audio take up, they have to be compressed—often using a technology called MPEG4.

Your videos might seem a little jerky while recording and playing back, and this is where it's worth checking the frames per second (fps) rate of your handset. Usually, video is recorded and played back at 25fps, and movies at 24fps. However, often mobiles can only manage between 10 and 20fps, but that is improving all the time.

Here are 10 videomaking tips for your mobile.

1. Keep clips short. This increases their impact and reduces audience boredom.

2. Keep movement as smooth as possible. It's difficult to watch jerky footage.

3. Avoid shooting subjects at long distances, your phone's lens isn't powerful enough, or the screen big enough!

4. Try shooting from different angles. Vary the height and position of your shot.

5. If you have a zoom don't overuse it. Move closer to your subject

6. If you can, plan in advance what you're recording. This way you'll see if what you want is achievable before it's too late.

7. Mix up shot sizes. Try getting close-ups, instead of trying to fit everything in the frame.

8. Your phone's built-in microphone is not as good as its image quality. You need to be near the sound source to record it properly.

9. Be inventive! Your cellphone is smaller than every film camera, and it can get into places they can't.

10. Be ruthless when editing. Don't be afraid to lose footage that looks good, but doesn't help tell the story.

When it comes to storing and exporting footage, it's fair to say that you're not going to get a lot of video clips on the storage cards you get with your phone, so it's worth investing in extra capacity cards. There is a range of cards, for different manufacturers' handsets, on the market, and they include SD, MMC, MS Duo, and mini-SD. Capacities can go up to 1GB—and using MPEG4 compression that equals a lot of video footage.

To get the footage off the camera you can use USB connections to a PC, Bluetooth wireless technology, or you could invest in a media card reader. These are available for single types of media (e.g. SD), or multiformat readers are also available.

Many of the latest phones are as much sophisticated cameras and media centers as they are devices for making voicecalls.

Smartphones and 3G phones save on carrying bulky or expensive video equipment around with you when you go on vacation.

In terms of editing, some handsets allow you to trim video clips on the handset itself. However for even better results you should look to get the footage off your phone and onto a PC.

Muvee Technologies has partnered with Nokia, and its Movie Director software is now bundled with many of the company's handsets. This allows you to cut up your clips, add titles and a new soundtrack, plus a few special effects and scene transitions (fades, dissolves, etc). Muvee also has an application called AutoProducer for Windows XP operating systems, which enables you to edit your footage and then burn it to VideoCD (VCD) or DVD, so you can send a copy of your masterpiece to friends and family.

Ulead's Video ToolBox 2 software has a Home Edition for 3G cellphones. Using a PC, you can import and edit your clips in formats such as AVI, MPEG1, MPEG2, MPEG4, and Windows Media (WMV) and you can then output to 3GPP/3GPP2, the most common formats for mobile video.

It's also worthwhile paying a visit to www.handango.com. This company is a provider of mobile downloads, and has a massive array of applications on offer, for common operating systems, such as: Windows Mobile, Pocket PC, Palm OS, Symbian OS, Blackberry, Windows Mobile Smartphone, Linux, and Tablet PC.

Video Capture

What's on a Camcorder?
There is a wide variety of features that you'll find on virtually every camcorder. Here are some of the key functions, and what you might use them for.

001 On automatic

You can use Automatic controls to make shooting your video easier. The camcorder will take care of major controls such as Focus and Exposure to make sure your video looks as good as possible. This is especially useful if you haven't got time to switch on and set any Manual controls.

002 Manual labor

Use Manual controls when you can, as you can make amendments and corrections to your video as you go, so that the scene is sharp and the color levels look right. Using Manual controls takes longer to master, but they give you more creative control.

003 Zoom control

The Zoom control can often be overused by beginners. It's great for getting close-ups, but zooming in and out too often can make your video difficult to watch. Whenever you can, try moving closer to your subject rather than zooming in.

004 Screenplay

Every digital camcorder has some sort of LCD screen. The screen serves two purposes; you might use it to frame the footage you're about to record, or you can use the screen to watch and review the video you've just shot.

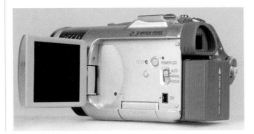

005 Conserving power

LCD screens use up more battery power than viewfinders, so if you need to conserve power, switch off the screen. Luckily, most camcorders will have an onscreen indicator telling you how much battery power is left.

007 In view

The majority of digital camcorders also feature a viewfinder, as well as an LCD screen. This small eyepiece can be used to compose shots. Color and black-and-white versions are available.

010 Going steady

There are times when you're holding the camcorder in your hand and you just can't keep it steady enough. Use an Image Stabilizer to help you smooth out these shakes. The camcorder automatically compensates for small amounts of unnecessary movement. This rarely results in any drop in image quality.

006 Screen size

LCD screen sizes range from $1^3/_4$ to $3^1/_2$ inches (4.5–9cm). Remember: screens are measured diagonally to give this figure.

008 View point

Black-and-white viewfinders are favored by experienced videomakers as they give a better representation of contrast and exposure levels.

009 Sound bite

Digital camcorders record digital sound, too. There are generally two sound recording types: PCM and Dolby Digital. Both methods are stereo, and usually offer the chance to record—or Audio Dub as it's known—a new soundtrack over existing video.

011 Lighting-up time

For scenes when the background is very bright and the foreground looks so dark you can hardly see any detail, the Backlight Compensation function is a great effect. Use this function to reduce the brightness of the background and bring out detail in the foreground. As the videomaker you'll get a much more attractive shot.

012 The go-between

An effective compromise between shooting on fully Automatic or fully Manual modes, are Program AE (autoexposure) modes. These are available on all digital camcorders. They are Exposure, White Balance, and Shutter Speeds specifically preset for certain conditions, for example: Beach and Ski, Sand and Snow, Low Light, Sports, and Spotlight.

013 Making a move

Getting video and sound off your camcorder onto a computer is very straightforward. Depending on your computer connections, you can use FireWire or USB. Both methods transfer large amounts of data very quickly, and once on your computer you can start editing.

014 In and out

FireWire can be used to transfer images and sound from your camcorder to a computer. This is known as DV-out. Some camcorders have a DV-in/out, meaning you can also send images and sound back to your camcorder. FireWire is often referred to as IEEE-1394 or DV-in/out, but it is all the same thing.

015 Digital stills

Many camcorders can now save digital still images as well as digital video. This is very easy to do, as your camcorder will have a Photo button. These are usually a different shape to the Record button so you can't mistake the two.

016 Microphone sockets

Sometimes you might need to plug in an external microphone if you need professional-quality sound. Not all digital camcorders have a mic socket, so check this out first. Likewise, headphone sockets aren't on all models, but they're especially useful for monitoring the sound your camcorder is recording.

HOW TO BUY A CAMCORDER

019 Set a budget

Decide on your budget. Being realistic will help you make the right decision, as digital camcorders can cost as little as $150, or up to several thousand dollars.

017 Manual focus

A Manual Focus Ring is found around the lens barrel on more expensive digital camcorders aimed at enthusiasts. The Ring rotates around the lens, and enables you to set the Focus manually.

018 Old meets new

Analog inputs might sound like a weird idea but they can be immensely useful. They allow an analog device such as a VCR to be connected to the camcorder. It's possible to record analog video onto digital tape, disk, or hard drive. Great for transferring old analog tapes, or even recording programs from the TV!

020 Check compatibility

Choose a recording format, and decide why. Consider the equipment you already have, and make sure your camcorder will work with it... or you'll be spending a lot of extra money on more new equipment to watch your videos!

021 Your needs

Decide what features you need to have, and those you can really live without. This will help you fix your budget, and decide what kind of videomaker you'll be.

022 On test

Touch and try. Always test out a digital camcorder before buying it. At the very least, you should know how it feels to hold and whether you think it's comfortable.

024 3CCDs

What is a 3CCD camcorder? The majority of camcorders feature just one CCD (Charge Coupled Device) that turns signals into images. 3CCD models offer greater picture quality, but invariably see a rise in price. Definitely worth considering if you want to make more accomplished movies, but not essential.

023 Size matters

Does size matter? In terms of the size of a camcorder, yes it does! It's not that bigger models are better, it's just that smaller ones can be difficult for some people to operate. Buttons can be small and unresponsive on certain models, and there's simply no point having a camcorder that you don't like to use.

025 Edit for free

It's very likely you'll get editing software free with your digital camcorder. This can be used to transfer video, audio, and still images off your camcorder onto a computer, and can even let you create DVDs. Check your computer system first for compatibility.

ESSENTIAL ACCESSORIES

If you want to get the most out of your camcorder, it's worth investing in a few extra "toys" to help you. There's an amazing array of accessories on offer, but only a few that are really essential. Here are some of the options.

026 Tripods

The three-legged support you get from a tripod is the best way to shoot rock-solid images. Look out for sturdy build quality and smooth movement, both up and down, and side to side from the head of the tripod. Some tripods have a built-in spirit level so you can be sure your shots are level.

028 Extra storage

Whichever format you record on, it's vital that you have extra capacity with you when you're shooting. Try to have spare tapes, DVDs, or memory cards with you whenever possible.

029 Cleaners

A quick dab at your camcorder's lens with an optical cleaning cloth can save you the heartache of watching your footage and realizing you have a stray hair in every single frame!

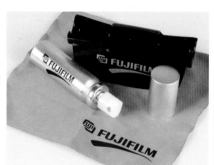

030 Going undercover

You'd be amazed at how many people invest several hundred dollars in a digital camcorder, but don't think about buying a cover to protect it when shooting in the rain. Don't be amazed—just be sensible!

027 Spare batteries

Having at least one spare, charged battery is essential if you're out and about. That way it's quick and easy to swap over, and you might not miss that classic scene. It's also good to have a stash of several batteries if you're going to do a lot of recording.

031 Skylight Filters

A skylight filter keeps your lens from getting scratched by sand or damaged by dirt but doesn't do anything to alter your images. Filters are available in different sizes to fit your camcorder, and are screwed in front of the lens.

033 Microphones

Your camcorder has a built-in microphone, but sometimes it's not so adept at picking up precisely the sounds you want. If you want top-quality audio, look at investing in an external microphone. These can be plugged into a socket on your camcorder (if it has one). Mics can be directional (recording sound from one direction), bidirectional, or omnidirectional.

032 Light Filters

A Neutral Density filter is also essential. It reduces the amount of light entering the camcorder's lens, but doesn't affect the way colors are recorded. It's great for using in very bright conditions, like at the beach or when skiing. A valuable addition to your kit if you know you're going to be shooting a video on vacation—and don't forget to plan for those changing seasons!

034 Headphones

If your camcorder has a headphone socket, use it! Camcorders don't "hear" sound like we do, they just record everything. Listening to exactly what your microphone is recording using a set of headphones helps avoid sound problems in the long-run.

ACCESSORY CHECKLIST

- Tripod
- Spare batteries
- Spare tapes/disks
- Lens/cleaning cloth
- Lens or camcorder cover
- Skylight filter
- Neutral Density filter
- External microphone
- Headphones
- Bag

035 Carrying your equipment

So, you have all these accessories... what are you going to carry them in? Consider the size and weight of your extras before buying a bag or case, and make sure that whatever you buy offers plenty of support and cushioning for all that delicate equipment.

Technique

Videomaking is not just about the equipment—a good director can shoot worldbeating footage with the right technique, even if the hardware is not the best that money can buy. Here are some basic dos, don'ts, and professional observations.

THE BASIC RULES OF VIDEOMAKING

036 Following guidelines

A videomaking friend of mine once started a talk on an aspect of the filming process by saying: "There are no rules in videomaking." In his very next sentence he used the phrase: "One of the most important rules you must learn is...."

It's understandable how a beginner can feel there are too many essentials to grasp. Remember: most "rules" are really technical "good practice" guides rather than stylistic imperatives.

038 Be selective

Don't feel like you have to record every single moment and event. The best home movies come when you pick the moving, funny, or dramatic moments. Hone your eye by being selective from the outset—and save yourself an editing job later!

037 The lingo

The filmmakers' language is useful to learn when making your own home movies. Once you understand the lingo, then you'll be far more comfortable with what to do and how to do it. Make notes of every technical term you come across in this book and learn it—it's part of the fun, and it will help you think yourself into the role of director and cameraman.

039 Keep it brief

Keep the length of each clip you take down to a minimum. The human eye can process a lot of information very quickly, so you don't have to record in long chunks.

SHOT SIZES

 Taking the long shot

A scene usually begins with a long shot (LS). This is because it's the best way of setting the scene. For example, you might begin a vacation video with a long shot of your resort, showing off the long sandy beaches and dazzling views.

042 Close-ups

The next logical step is to add a close-up (CU). This can add even more information, or help focus attention on one particular character—such as the star of your video. Here, you would move closer to your subject, but also use the zoom to get really "tight in" (closely focused) on your main subject: hands, faces, flowers, etc.

043 Zoom with caution

A word on zooming. Overusing the zoom is the most common "mistake" made by beginners. It's not really a mistake though, just a technique that can make it difficult for people to watch your movie. If you want a closer look at something, wherever possible just move closer to it.

044 Add variety

There are variations to all the shot sizes we've mentioned. So you could shoot an extreme close-up (ECU) if you wanted to. This might disorientate your viewer, but then in a nice twist you could use the next shot to zoom out and show what you're looking at.

041 Medium shot

After a long shot you might often cut to a medium shot (MS). This gives a closer look at the action, and offers the viewer more information. So, taking our vacation video one step further, you might choose to look more closely at the vacationers sunning themselves, or buying their ice creams.

VIDEOMAKING TERMS

045 Your "frame"

When referring to your "frame," we mean what you can see when you look through the viewfinder, or what you can see on the LCD screen. What you include in the frame is a matter of taste, but can dramatically influence story, character, understanding, and enjoyment.

047 Background

The area at the rear of your video frame is known as the background. Explore the different effects of using it as a visual context for whatever happens in the foreground or center, and as a storytelling device, by setting a scene with the action in the background—and then moving in to find your characters.

048 Center ground

The area in the middle of your video frame is known as the center, and is usually where the majority of the action, or interest, in your video takes place.

046 Foreground

The area at the front of your video frame is known as the foreground. Explore its use by filling it with something, by setting a scene with the action taking place in the background, or as a framing device for action that's happening in the center ground.

049 A cut-in shot

A cut-in can be seen as just another close-up shot. But using it helps you, the videomaker, to tell a story. For example, you have a man walking along the street with a bag. You then have a close-up of the bag. You then film a cut-in of the man reaching inside the bag, and can focus on exactly what's in the bag.

050 Cutaways

Cutaways are great for adding a bit of extra interest to a video, or for helping to tell the story. They're often not essential, but do still have to be related to the story. Your character waits for a friend outside a station. To indicate that someone's running late, you can film a cutaway of a clock to tell the audience what the time is.

051 Panning

Moving the camcorder sideways is known as a pan. So, if you were asked to pan right, you would move the camcorder smoothly toward the right.

052 Tilting

A tilt is when you move the camcorder either up or down. Use this with care and with purpose to avoid disorienting the viewer.

053 Pull-focus shots

You'll need to use manual focus to achieve a pull-focus shot, but they're great for adding emphasis to a video. Using the manual focus, you can make the foreground go fuzzy (out of focus), and the audience will then concentrate on the center or background areas. Or vice versa—make the background fuzzy to emphasize your foreground interest.

054 Jump cuts

Jump cuts are a brilliant example of how there aren't really many firm videomaking rules. Traditionally, a jump cut was seen as a filmmaker's mistake, where one scene doesn't run smoothly with what follows it.

055 Jump 1

Your first shot sees Dad on vacation, walking toward the camcorder. Dad's about 20 feet (6m) away.

056 Jump 2

Dad's walking toward you as you film, but you don't record him walking all the way up to you. Instead, you only record him for a couple of seconds.

057 Jump 3

In your next shot, Dad's miraculously leapt about 15 feet (5.5m). This is because he kept walking while you'd stopped filming. Dad is now almost upon the camcorder. It looks like he's jumped a large distance in a short time. You have inadvertently created a jump cut.

058 Be creative

Dad's comical jump is a mistake, but what if you were trying to be funny? Now your jump cut is intentional, and you're breaking the rules of video... in a good way, because it's creative!

059 Lead room

Lead room is the space you leave in front of your subject for them to move into. Mom skis into shot from the right, and leaves on the left. You should record with space in front of her all the way through the shot.

060 Tracking

A tracking shot is one that involves moving the camcorder to keep the subject in the frame. This will be because your subject (person, car, etc) is moving.

FRAMING

061 Plan a shot

Once you have your camcorder up and running, you shouldn't necessarily just press the record button. Always try to find time to think about what you're going to record, and how you're going to do it.

062 Test run

There's no harm in doing a test run of what you're going to record. You can practice taking the shot, without recording it to tape.

063 Composition

Composition is one of the key elements behind getting a great-looking home movie. If you learn a few handy techniques you can make even the most ordinary situations look more interesting.

064 Rule of thirds

The rule of thirds is essential knowledge. Imagine a grid dividing your image into horizontal and vertical thirds (nine squares). To balance what will be competing elements in your shot, attempt to place your subjects on the grid intersections–or devote two thirds of the screen to one element, and a third to another.

065 Using zoom

A few more words on zooming: it is not forbidden to use the zoom! You can use it to help frame a shot that you want a close-up of. Or you can zoom smoothly to focus attention on a particularly interesting aspect of the video.

066 Crash zoom

If you want to be more creative, you can use what's known as a crash zoom. This is where you zoom in or out at a fast speed. It's fantastic for jazzing up footage, and is used a lot in music videos. Remember to test it out before shooting, as you want to be able to zoom in on the right thing!

067 Framing tip

When framing a subject, especially when this is a person, try to have the bottom of the screen fall midway between joints. A shot that stops at the elbow looks stranger than one that ends at the forearm.

068 Cutting it

A common framing mistake can see you cutting off the top of someone's head, or lopping off their feet.

069 A cut above

If you're being creative, you can deliberately cut off the top of someone's head. Say, for example you want to zoom in closer during an interview. The secret is to ensure that it looks deliberate. Many photographers shoot portraits that crop out part of the subject's head to create more dynamic compositions.

070 Spice up long shots

A long shot might look a bit dull without anything else in the frame. Try adding some foreground interest, without distracting from the main focus of the shot.

071 All natural

Most locations will provide you with natural framing aids. Trees and plants are useful for helping to frame a shot, and to add extra interesting elements.

072 Make your own

More than a few professional videomakers "cheat" and have a colleague hold branches in shot, to help frame the shot more attractively.

073 Perspective

You might remember perspective from art class. In videomaking, it's vital for creating depth, texture, angles, and for a better-looking video. Instead of filming your subject head-on, which can look flat and boring, try changing the angle. You can then give the viewer more information.

WHAT IS DEPTH OF FIELD?

074 Acceptable focus

When your lens is focused on a specific point, there'll be a distance in front of, as well as behind, that specific point, which will also be in acceptable focus. This area of acceptable focus is known as depth of field.

075 Thinking in thirds

One third of the depth of field area is in front of your focal point, and two thirds is behind it.

076 Zooming in

The depth of field (amount of frame in acceptable focus) decreases as the focal length increases. When you zoom in, less of the frame is in acceptable focus.

CAMERA PLACEMENT, ANGLES, AND EYELINES

077 Positioning

Where you place the camcorder is very important. Place it away from the action, and your audience will feel like observers. Place it in among the action, and the audience will feel like they're involved.

079 Areas of light and shadow

If you don't have the chance to visit a location before you film there, such as when you're on vacation or at a party, then look for areas with light and shadow.

080 Color and interest

If you can't always find light, look for bright or vibrant colors and for interesting locations. These might have odd lighting, or the room itself might be an odd shape.

078 Thinking ahead

Always consider where your next shot might be. If you start with a long shot showing the entire scene, will your second shot be a close-up giving lots of detail, or covering a telling look or glance?

081 Scout around

If you can research a location before filming, a wedding being a prime example, make sure you do. This will provide invaluable information on where you can set up your camcorder, and where you might need to go for handheld shooting.

082 Seek permission

When visiting a location—again a wedding is top of the list—just take time to make sure it's alright with the people concerned that you can film there.

083 Filming in public places

Filming on the street is usually not a problem, provided you don't create a disturbance. However, public transport systems and public buildings (such as museums and galleries) might only allow you to film if you've applied for a permit.

085 Level-headed

Many beginners simply switch on the camcorder, put it up to their eye and start recording. If you did this all the time, all your shots would be from exactly the same height... and that would look monotonous.

084 Angle adjustment

Using a variety of camera angles will make your video more exciting and interesting to watch. Different camera angles can also help you to tell a story better because they can add extra information.

086 Vary the filming height

Try recording from different heights. Shots from high angles can give a great view looking down on crowd scenes. Low angles, close to the ground, can seem closer to the action—brilliant for when cars or bikes go zipping past.

087 Point of view

A point of view (POV) shot does what it says on the tin: it's filmed as if you're looking through the eyes of your subject. You're seeing what they're seeing.

088 Shooting up

When shooting scenes like an interview or a piece direct to the camcorder, looking up at the subject usually imparts respect.

089 Shooting down

Shooting a similar scene, but recording while looking down at the subject can reduce their stature, or just make them actually look a lot smaller!

090 Shooting straight on

If you're not sure which of the above angles to take, settle for recording them straight in the eye.

091 Talking direct to camera

You don't want a person on-camera reading something (like a narration) that's off-camera. This will be unsettling for the viewer, who will feel that the person is being evasive. Get your narrator to learn their lines!

092 Make your mind up

If your subject isn't supposed to look directly at the camcorder, then tell them. It is unnerving for an audience to suddenly have a character gazing directly at them. Alternatively, if you're making a fiction movie, this trick can be used to grab the viewers' attention.

093 Eye to eye

If you want an audience to realize that two people are looking at each other when you've shot them separately, their eyelines must match. If one character is looking up, then the corresponding character must be looking down.

094 Playing with eyelines

You can play with eyelines to help inject drama or comedy into a scene. For example, if one character is looking directly at another, but the other character is looking away, this could be used to suggest an argument, anger, or even someone being coy and bashful.

095 Give plenty of detail

Try to give your audience as much detail as possible. In interview situations an Over-the-Shoulder-Two-Shot is commonly used. This is simply a shot taken from behind the interviewer, showing that two (or more) people are involved in the scene.

096 30° (or 30%) rule

When there isn't enough variety between shots, you are breaking the 30° (or 30%) rule. Make sure that when you move the camcorder you do so by 30°. Or, if you change the framing (by zooming), then change it by at least 30%.

097 Panning & tilting

Practice pans and tilts in advance, not only so that you can ensure you record what you want to, but also to make certain that you have room to do it, and feel comfortable.

098 Take it slow

A pan or tilt should be done slowly and smoothly. This gives the viewer's eyes enough time to follow the action. When watching movement, our eyes naturally dart ahead of the action.

099 On track

Follow the action with a tracking shot. In movies, pros use a wheeled device called a dolly. You can improvize. Ensure whatever you use runs smoothly, so you don't get unwanted bumps. A wheelchair, shopping cart, or wheeled trashcan are all useful!

100 A beginning and an end

Give every shot that includes movement—whether it's panning, tilting, or tracking—a beginning and an end. Otherwise, the shot will look rootless, and confuse the audience.

CROSSING THE LINE

101 Improve your filming

The crossing the line rule may seem difficult to grasp at first, but the good news is that once you've got it, you won't have to think about it. And, perhaps more importantly, you'll get much better-looking home movies out of it. Master the following rule.

102 Imagine a line

It's known as crossing the line, because you need to imagine a line between your subjects, and to always stay on one side of it.

103 Keep to the same side

Crossing the line is about making things clear for your audience. Imagine watching sport on TV: basketball is a good example. You can see that one team is attacking the basket toward the left of your screen, and the other is attacking the right. This looks natural, because the cameras following the action always follow it from the same side—so, the team attacking left will always look to be attacking that way.

104 Crossing causes confusion

Imagine if the cameras moved without warning, and started filming the game from the other side of the court. The team that was attacking left would now appear to be attacking right. You would feel confused, and find it more difficult to follow the game. If the cameras kept switching to different sides of the court, you'd have no idea which side was attacking which basket.

105 On track

OK, more examples. If you filmed a horse race and stood so the horses ran past you, right to left, but then you moved to the opposite side of the track, so the horses now raced past you left to right, you'd be confused as to which direction the horses were running in when you came to watch that footage.

106 Band aid

You're watching a DVD of your favorite band in concert. The band is always on stage looking out to the audience, and the audience is always in the auditorium looking toward the band on stage. Cross the line, and that natural state will be altered.

107 Chat show

Final example. If you cross the line on a shot of two people chatting, you'll end up with the two people facing the same way. If you don't give your audience any more details, they'll end up thinking that the two people aren't talking to each other at all.

It's vital to cut between shots logically and consistently when dealing with two or more characters. Mixing up the directions from which characters are shot will confuse the viewer and destroy the narrative. Cutting from one to the other from a consistent viewpoint will establish the narrative and lead the viewer into the story.

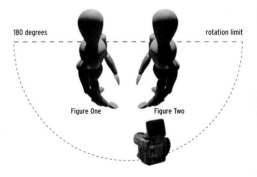

180 degrees   rotation limit

Figure One   Figure Two

A WORD ON WIDESCREEN

108 Watch the pros

It's probably fair to say that if you're interested in making home movies, you're also a bit of a film fan. Whether watching on TV or at the local multiplex, there's always something you can learn from seeing the professionals at work.

109 16:9 aspect ratio

A cinema screen has what's called an aspect ratio of 16:9. This means it is wider than it is high. Think of a group of square boxes, stacked nine high and 16 across.

110 Widescreen format

The 16:9 aspect ratio is often referred to as widescreen or letterbox format, because the rectangular shape resembles the dimensions of a letterbox.

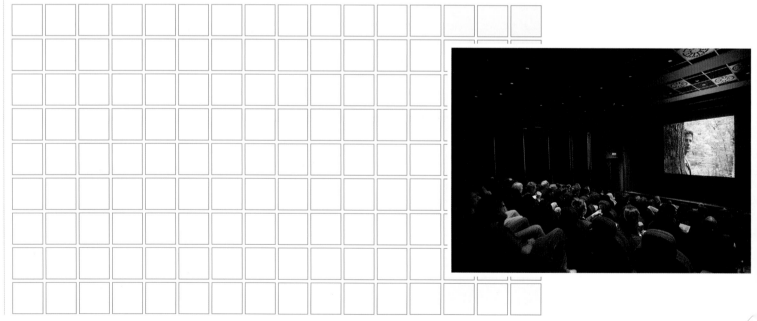

111 4:3 aspect ratio

Traditionally, TVs have had an aspect ratio of 4:3, which is more of a square than the rectangular shape of the 16:9 ratio. However, the popularity of widescreen TVs has changed this, allowing videomakers to screen their work in a widescreen (16:9) format.

112 Mimic widescreen

But what about if you actually want to record your home videos in widescreen? Well, most digital camcorders offer this function, too. There is a variety of settings available. A cinema mode can often place black bars at the top and bottom of the frame to mimic widescreen ratio, but the top and bottom of your frame will be cut off.

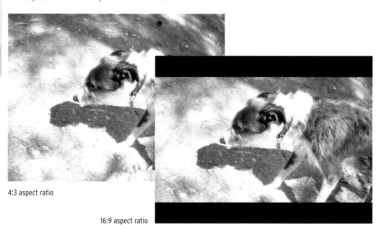

4:3 aspect ratio

16:9 aspect ratio

113 Putting on the squeeze

A squeeze mode will allow you to record footage that appears squashed up when you show it on a 4:3 TV. When you screen it on a widescreen television, it will fill the screen and look natural.

114 Shooting in widescreen

Camcorders toward the higher end of the consumer market can actually record true 16:9 widescreen images, so there's no squashing, squeezing, or letterboxing going on.

115 Framing as widescreen

Many digital camcorders now include LCD screens that have an aspect ratio closer to that of widescreen, so you can even frame your videos using the 16:9 ratio.

Working with Equipment

There are thousands of potentially useful accessories and gadgets that can be used with your camcorder to make your shots better or more interesting. Here, we'll cover how to get the best daily use out of the most important gear. Don't worry if you don't fancy buying more equipment–at the end of the section we'll show you how to create some excellent shots and equipment using little more than household objects and ingenuity.

TRIPODS & MONOPODS

Shaky camerawork is often the province of arty films or gritty TV drama, and it can work well in the right circumstances, but most of the time you're going to want your shots to look smooth and steady, and a tripod or monopod is vital for this.

116 Tripods

As we've already covered, a tripod is the most useful accessory you can buy as it allows you to get rock-steady shots from a variety of angles and heights. But before going out shopping for a tripod, check your camcorder manual to see how much your camcorder weighs, then check that the tripod you're after will support the weight.

117 Cash conscious

Tripods range in price from incredibly inexpensive models to ones costing hundreds of dollars, adorned with all sorts of gadgets and mechanical capabilities. The best ones are actually sold in separate parts–head and legs– allowing you to mix and match what you need.

118 Buy carefully

Before you set out to buy a tripod, think about how seriously you intend to take your shooting. We'd recommend that everyone invest in a tripod, but if you're only going to shoot once or twice a year, don't be seduced by the fully-featured expensive models. Look instead for something cheap. It's easy to think that because you've bought an expensive camcorder you need an expensive tripod to do it justice–but that's rarely true.

119 Think about the weight

If you're going to be doing intensive shots with a crew, you'll probably have someone to help carry equipment and can therefore afford a heavier and more durable tripod,. But if it's just you, then look for something lighter. Try to find one that comes with a bag, as the strange shape of a collapsed tripod makes it hard to match bag to job.

120 Head type

The two main types of head are pan-and-tilt, and ball-and-socket. Pan-and-tilt heads offer steady left-to-right and up-and-down angles, and are stable. For a wider range of angles, or when shooting subjects where you have to follow a lot of movement, the free motion of a ball-and-socket head offers more flexibility, but is also likely to cost more.

121 Pan handling

A pan bar is a handle that allows you to move the camera left and right, or tilt it up and down, whilst retaining the stability of the tripod.

122 Spirits and measures

Most tripod heads have a spirit level built in so you can adjust the various planes of the head until the camera is dead level. This is very useful on rocky or uneven terrain where your eyes might not be the best guide.

123 Center columns

Adjustable center columns can be wound up and down with a handle, allowing you to adjust the height of the camcorder without having to adjust the legs of the tripod.

124 Quick release

Most camcorders screw onto a thread on the tripod head, but many tripods have this thread mounted on a quick-release platform that can be quickly clipped into the head, allowing you to save time when changing cameras or tapes.

125 Spread 'em!

Leg spreaders, despite their dubious-sounding name, can add rigidity to your tripod when it's in use, and make the whole setup more stable, so there's less chance of an accidental nudge against one leg toppling the whole setup.

126 Remote control

If you want to avoid even the slightest wobble to your footage, you can invest in a Lanc controller. These plug into your camcorder's Lanc socket and then attach to the pan bar of your tripod, and have record and zoom controls on them, allowing you to operate the camcorder without touching it.

127 Tiny tripods

If you want stability but can't justify the expense of even a cheap tripod, look for a table tripod. These are usually 6-12 inches (15-30.5cm) high, and cost less than a pack of DV tapes. They can be propped on any flat surface and used to steady your camcorder, and can also be used as a pistol-grip when shooting handheld, which will make your shots smoother.

129 Stabilizers

Tripods and monopods are all very well when the camcorder is stationary, but if you want smooth shots whilst moving the camcorder you need a stabilizer. These work like professional steadicams, by isolating the camcorder from your movements and counterbalancing it with several weights.

130 Balancing act

Stabilizers consist of a camcorder platform attached to a free-floating handle that soaks up the jarring of your footsteps. Stabilizers take some getting used to, as you have to carefully counterbalance the weight of your cam using the weights that come with the stabilizer, and you have to learn how to move in a way that allows the platform to float properly. Once you master this, however, you'll be able to carry out stunning tracking shots.

128 Going mono

Sometimes you won't have enough room for a tripod, in which case you can use a monopod. Monopods have only one leg and need to be held. They aren't as steady as tripods but are still much smoother than shooting by hand. They're also lighter, cheaper, much more portable, and can be used like a pistol grip to stabilize your camcorder even when not braced against the ground.

CAMCORDER COVERS, CASES, AND BAGS

Your camcorder is an expensive and fragile piece of equipment, and it's important to look after
it properly. You can just sling it in any old bag, but then it will just rattle around as you walk,
collide with other equipment in the bag, and eventually end up battered and needing repair.
Even when in use, sometimes your camcorder will need protection from a case or cover.

131 Hard-shell

A hard-shelled case made of durable plastic is ideal if you've got a really large and
expensive camcorder that need lots of space and protection. Hard-shelled cases are
solid enough on the outside to resist even heavy blows, while the inside is usually
made up of foam padding cut into cubes. Whatever size or shape of equipment you
have can be fitted into the case just by removing the right amount of cubes from the
right places. The drawback to hard-shell cases is that they're heavy and cumbersome.
If your equipment doesn't justify a hard-shell, look for a camera bag instead.

132 Bag it up

Camera bags come in all shapes and sizes,
from large holdalls to rucksacks, or simple
pouches for a small camcorder on its
own. When looking at camera
bags, remember that it will
need to hold at least a few spare
tapes, batteries, and a charger as
well as your camcorder.

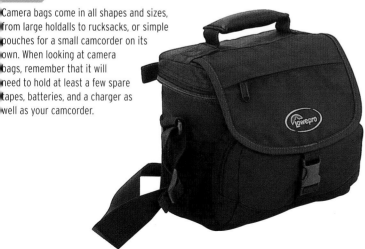

133 Padding the part

Unlike an ordinary bag, a camera bag will have lots of padding to
protect whatever you put in there. Check that the bag you're
buying feels like it will look after your kit. We've learnt through
expensive experience that not everything that calls itself a
camera bag is actually padded enough to prevent breakages.

134 It's what's inside that counts

In addition to padded walls, make
sure you choose a bag that has
interior padded compartments
to protect individual pieces of
equipment. It's no good buying
a bag that protects your kit
from the outside but lets
everything bash together
on the inside. Many bags
have moveable internal
padding that can be
velcroed into new
positions, allowing
you to create specific
padded compartments
for different pieces
of equipment.

135 Whatever the weather

Make sure your bag is waterproof as well as padded, especially if you're going to use it outdoors or on vacation. Check that the flaps on the bag are large enough to fully cover the openings in case of rainy weather, or invest in a bag that has a built-in rain cover.

136 Open up

Easy access is vital, as you'll be kicking yourself if you're still rummaging around while something important happens. Many camcorder bags have a springy opening system made of flexible flaps that close to a zipper's width when not in use but instantly pop wide open when you want them to.

137 Strappy little number

If you're going to use a tripod or monopod, look for a bag that has external straps which will let you securely attach the tripod bag or any other equipment you want to it, leaving your hands free.

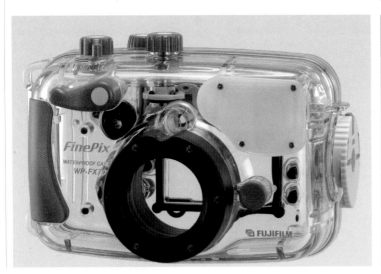

138 The virtue of subtlety

Try to get a camcorder bag that isn't bright and colorful or needlessly overdesigned. The more noticeable a camera bag is, the more it screams "steal me" to any opportunistic passerby. A camcorder bag that looks like an ordinary gym bag or backpack is much safer. If your kitbag does turn out to be rather eye-catching, put it in an ordinary gym bag to disguise it.

139 Rain capes

The sou'wester for camcorders, rain capes are essentially plastic bags that fit over the top of your camcorder and hang part way down your arm, providing complete protection from a sudden downpour. Where they differ from your average supermarket carrier bag is in the integrated lens fitting. The cape has a hard plastic ring into which the lens barrel of your camcorder fits, and the ring has a clear plastic disk that won't interfere with your camcorder lens, allowing you to completely shroud the camcorder yet still be able to shoot. Rain capes are vital if you're going to use your camcorder outdoors frequently, and are available in a range of sizes for all makes and models.

140 Underwater protection

Aqua or scuba housings are the ultimate in camcorder protection, and are priced accordingly. Completely watertight, incredibly durable, and slightly shockproof, the housings have replicated controls on the outside that allow the camcorder to be operated despite being completely sealed-up. This means that you have to buy the exact housing that matches your camcorder model. It's not an expense we'd recommend unless you're certain you're going to use it, but if you want to try your hand at beautiful underwater photography, you'll need one of these.

FILTERS AND LENS CONVERTERS

Most camcorders have all sorts of features built-in to change the look of your footage or to cope with adverse shooting conditions such as heavy backlighting. However, sometimes you might find you need something that's not already built-in, which is where filters come in.

141 Filters

Filters are plastic or glass disks that attach to the front of your camcorder and affect the light that enters the lens. They range from ones that alter the quality of the light for better pictures in adverse conditions to those that actually create a specific visual effect.

142 Threads

The lens of almost every camcorder has a filter diameter. This is the size of the thread into which you screw a filter. Look at your camcorder lens–the diameter symbol is a circle with a diagonal line through it. The figure attached to this symbol is the size of filter to shop for.

143 Stepping rings

If you can't find the filter you need in the correct size, you can buy a stepping ring. This has two different-sized threads, one to attach a filter to, and the other to attach to your camcorder.

144 Put it in neutral

Neutral density filters are the most commonly used type of filter. They have a gray appearance and are used to reduce the amount of light passing through the lens without affecting color or contrast values. They're useful for regulating uneven lighting conditions and for allowing you to increase depth of field with a wide aperture setting without losing control of your image exposure.

145 Skylight

A skylight filter comes in handy at sporting events or on vacation. It actually has no effect on the image and is essentially just a protective piece of glass that shields your lens from errant softballs or beach sand.

146 Graduated Filters

Graduated filters have an effect that is graduated across the lens.
For example, they may have a blue tint that slowly fades
away to nothing part way down the lens. These are
used to enhance parts of images. Those photos
with the incredible blue skies for example–
do you really think the photographer
simply waited for that good a day?

147 Polarizing Filters

Polarizing filters are used primarily for reducing glare and
flare from reflective subjects, although they can also be used to
enhance it. A polarizing filter lets you film through windows or
water on sunny days. Where normally you'd get a blazing white
reflection, a polarizing filter will let you look through the glass
or the water.

148 Softeners

Softening lenses reduce the sharpness of an image slightly,
without throwing it completely out of focus. They are ideal for
portrait shots as they soften or remove minor blemishes
and wrinkles.

149 Wide-angle convertor

While your camcorder has a function for zooming into a subject,
it's rare that it will have a setting to widen your picture. For this,
you need a wide-angle convertor lens which screws onto the
filter thread. Up to a rating of about x0.5, they will give you a
wider picture area. Beyond that size, up to about x0.35, they will
start to have a more dramatic distorting effect called "fish eye,"
in which items at the edge of the frame appear to bend in
toward the center.

150 Vignetting

One small problem with attaching zoom or wide-angle convertor
lenses to camcorders is vignetting, in which the addition of length
to the lens barrel causes the camcorder to try to see through the
side of the filter, creating a tunnel vision effect. This can be
avoided by zooming slightly.

BASIC LIGHTING

Most basic shoots don't require any lighting, and it's possible that you'll never need to light your video. Having said that, your camcorder is, primarily, a tool for working with light, so it's important to know some of the basics of lighting just in case. Imagine you're asked to film someone's wedding, or an important presentation–if the lighting is bad, you need to know how to make it better.

151 Don't make your own

People often think that video or film lights can be made cheaply using garden lamps or security lights. This is a mistake, as these sort of lights aren't "balanced," and tend to have a tinge to them that, although unnoticeable to the naked eye, will definitely affect your video, resulting in "color casts." Natural light or proper video lights are the best sources of illumination to work with.

152 Redheads and blonds

The most commonly used type of video light is the redhead, also known as the focusing reflector. These have significantly more wattage than household bulbs, and are balanced to the same blueish tinge as natural light, rather than the more orange tinge of an ordinary bulb. Higher wattage focusing reflectors are known as "blonds."

153 When do you need to light something?

The simple answer, of course, is when it's too dark. But before you consider unpacking your bought or rented lighting gear, take a look around and see if you can avoid having to light things. Opening drapes or using a reflector to cast existing light where you want it is cheaper and saves time.

154 Key lighting

If you do need to light your scene, there are three main styles of lighting that can be used in different combinations. The first is the key light. This is your primary light source for what you're shooting, and is used to drive out darkness and place realistic shadows. This is where the terms low-key and high-key come from. Low-key lighting is of a lesser brightness and intensity than high-key. Your key light is usually shone from the front or front side of your subject.

155 Fill lighting

When your key light is placed, you'll probably find that the shadows it creates are more intense than you want, illuminating most of your subject perfectly, but creating a few shrouded patches, such as the eyes or nose. Your fill light is placed to the opposite angle of your key to fill these shadows, but is of a lesser intensity so as not to completely override the key. Often a good fill lighting effect can be achieved by facing the light away from the subject and bouncing it back toward the subject with a reflector.

156 Kicker lights

Lastly, you have the kicker. With your key and fill in position, it's possible that both subject and background are so evenly lit as to appear flat. The kicker brings some depth back in by "kicking" your subject out from the background. Usually placed low and to the rear of the subject, the kicker adds some light to the edges of your subject, making it more clearly defined from the background.

157 Three-point lighting

The use of key, fill, and kicker in conjunction is called three-point lighting, and is handy for almost any type of lighting situation. The concept can be used with more than three lights, or you can use two-point or single-point lighting in less demanding situations.

158 Safety first

Video lights, or luminaires, get extremely hot. Be very careful when handling them, and always make sure that the stands are stable and won't fall over. It's incredibly rare, but luminaires have been known to blow outwards, so look for ones with reinforced glass. For this reason, it's also considered good etiquette to place your hand in front of the lamp when you switch it on. Sounds crazy, but it does reassure and protect the people being lit.

159 Gels

Gels are flexible pieces of translucent plastic that fit over your lights. Normally you use a blue gel to give your light a similar color temperature to sunlight, but by using different colored gels, or combining many gels on a single light, you can create some very impressive light effects.

160 Reflectors

Reflectors are used to bounce light to where it's needed. Made of a reflective fabric, they normally fold down to a small and easily portable size. The most common reflectors are white/silver and white/gold. The white is a basic reflector used for bouncing light from the sun or a luminaire at your subject, while the silver or gold sides are used to alter the light quality as well as reflecting it. The gold "warms" the light the most.

161 Softbox

A softbox is used to spread and diffuse the light from a single source. Made of springy fabric, they collapse for easy packing. Fitted over a luminaire they will spread the light as well as soften it, producing even lighting conditions with mild shadows for a very natural look.

162 Barn doors

Barn doors are hinged metal flaps that fit onto your lights, allowing you to restrict the spread of the light without reducing its intensity. Using barn doors you can create a very directional light source.

163 Snoots

A snoot is a conical version of barn doors. You can restrict the diameter of the beam, allowing you to create a spotlight.

BASIC SOUND RECORDING

Good pictures are nice, but combined with good sound they become great. In this section we'll teach you the basics of recording good sound and tell you what equipment you might need if you want to get ambitious with your audio.

164 Audio dub

The first and easiest thing you can do to improve your camcorder sound is to use the audio dub facility present on all DV camcorders. Ordinarily, your cam records 16-bit audio onto two channels. By switching this to 12-bit, however, you leave a channel free onto which you can dub music or narration onto your tapes. Simply plug a microphone or a stereo/minidisk player into the mic socket on your camcorder, and select audio dub from the menu.

165 Headphones

If you're going to record separate sound to add to your video during editing, you'll want to invest in some good headphones to monitor your recording. Headphones can be either closed, which let in no external noise and are therefore better for monitoring, or open, which let you hear the world around you and are much safer for shooting when you're out and about.

166 Destination

You'll also need to think about where your sound is going to end up. Once upon a time separate audio was recorded onto tape, but these days far better results can be achived using minidisk or even MP3. We've heard excellent results produced on minidisk recorders and MP3 players, the results of which have the added advantage of being more easily transferred to your editing system than tape.

167 Shotgun

Of course, you'll also need to find the microphone best suited to your recording. Shotgun mics are long and thin and easy to use by hand or when attached to a boom. The pickup pattern on them captures sound mainly from the front, which means you'll get only the sound you point them at.

168 Cardioid

Cardioid mics are the most common variety, and have a heart-shaped pickup pattern where most sound is picked up from the front, but some is also taken from the sides. These are very handy for recording ambient noise that adds interest and authenticity to your soundtrack.

169 Lavalier

Lavalier mics are the ones you see on TV clipped to people's ties, and are therefore often called tie-clip mics. Brilliant for picking up speech, lavaliers can be very useful during long interviews or when recording monologues.

170 Get as close as possible

The most important rule for recording good sound is to get as close as possible to the source of the sound. The closer you are, the cleaner and louder the sound will be. If it's inconvenient to put the camcorder and its microphone close to your subject, then try to record the sound separately by having a mic much closer to the subject than the camera.

171 Boom

The best way of getting your mic close to your source is by using a boom. These are long poles (sometimes called fishing poles) with a mic on the end that can be held directly above the source of the sound while still being too high to appear in shot. It's easy to make a boom from a fishing pole or aluminum tubing if you want to save money.

172 Shield the mic from wind

Wind disturbance is the most common interference with your sound, with pops and rustles being recorded as the wind hits the mic. You can use a wind-cut mode to reduce this, but on most camcorders this involves switching to mono sound recording. Instead, keep the camcorder recording in stereo and purchase a windshield made from foam or fur that fits over your microphone.

173 Listen for disturbances

Your mind is very good at screening out extraneous noises picked up by your ears, but that's a talent your camcorder doesn't have. Listen extra hard when recording for all the background noises (airplanes, the hum of fluorescent lights, etc) that will be picked up by your microphone.

174 Tapped up

If you're planning to add sound to your video at the editing stage, it's important to be able to synch it with a visual cue. You might think that you'll just start the words when someone's lips start moving, but it will never match. Get someone to snap a clapper board shut or tap the top of the microphone in shot, and then line the sound up to the movement in post-production.

Audio- and video-editing software works on a timeline principle, showing every element of your work graphically. You can line up audio cues visually in your edit suite.

175 Go wild

Silence is rarely actually silence, and ambient noise is never easy to recreate. A wildtrack is sound recorded independently of your picture that has nothing to do with your story and is used for realistic video soundtrack. Even an empty room has certain acoustic properties—even if it's silent it still doesn't sound the same as it would if you simply shot it with the volume turned down. A wildtrack will capture these properties, or the general ambient noise of any location you shoot in, and when mixed with your video, will make it sound authentic.

What Can I Video?

Right, so you know what camcorder, accessories, and kit you should have. Here are a few ideas on what you might use all that precious stuff for.

VACATIONS

176 Which vacation?

There are a couple of main vacation scenarios. First is a break where you just want a record of your visit, and the second is a trip of a lifetime where you want to document as much as you can. The latter takes careful planning, and a lot of specialist equipment. Here, we're going to concentrate on the standard vacation.

177 Stick to the highlights

For an average family break, try to cut down the amount of equipment you take—you don't want it to rule your trip. You're trying to relax, remember. Try restricting yourself to recording the highlights, such as special days out.

178 Essential kit

The essential kit should include the camcorder, a few tapes, cards or disks, a couple of batteries (one can be charging while the other's in use), a mains charger, and a secure bag to keep it all in.

179 Check voltage

Check the voltage in use where you're on vacation, so you can use the charger to power up those batteries.

180 The tripod stays home

A tripod can be unnecessary baggage. Instead, try using natural supports such as walls, fences, and tables—not quite so adaptable, but better than carrying around awkward bags.

181 Insurance check

Check your home contents and vacation insurance polices. Is your camcorder covered, or will you need to take out separate cover? Most leading insurers will offer cover for specific costly items.

182 Do some groundwork

Consider what you're shooting, plan it in advance where possible, and keep shot lengths short for maximum impact. You don't need to document all seven or 14 days!

183 Add variety

Shooting into the sun will lead to overexposed or bleached-out looking shots when you're using the camcorder's auto settings. Look for areas of light and shade to give your video variety.

184 People, not places

Make sure you video friends and family doing activities. Videos of buildings and beaches can look a little dull. Vary the height and angle of shots to add interest to the video.

185 Visual clues

Use road and town signs as a visual reference. They can also act as impromptu titles for the video, so you don't have to add them later when you're editing.

WEDDINGS

186 The big day

A really difficult and important engagement, so plan everything you can down to the last detail. You won't have any spare time on the day.

187 Ask permission

As a matter of courtesy find out in advance that it's alright for you to set up your camcorder where you need to. Priests and officiators often have control over a ceremony venue.

A WEDDING SEQUENCE

188 Set the scene

Record guests as they congregate. Mix shots of people milling around outside and inside the venue, grab a few shots of nervous relatives, and do a few interviews with key figures.

189 Get in position

If you're recording the ceremony on just one camcorder, position it so that you can capture the action in one fluid movement.

190 Make an entrance

Here we are fixed on the entrance to the church, ready to capture the bride as she comes in.

191 Walk on by

Follow the bride as she comes down the aisle with her party and arrives at the altar to meet her groom. But do take care not to be the center of attention or to spoil the moment by getting in the way!

192 Create atmosphere

Find the time to grab a few reaction shots of the guests as they comment on the bride's dress. Close-ups of smiles and of the odd tear help to add atmosphere.

194 Stay with that shot

You should now be able to relax slightly and use the same shot to record the entire ceremony... bar the unexpected, of course!

193 The happy couple

Now it's time to focus on the ceremony, so make sure the position of your camcorder allows you to focus in on the happy couple and the priest or officiator.

195 Shifting focus

If you're allowed to, stick with the wedding party and record the signing of the register or official documents. If not, concentrate on atmospheric shots of the congregation. Mix up medium and close-up shots.

196 Change position

Change location and get to the exit of the church so that you can record the couple coming back down the aisle and leaving—much better than running down the aisle in the happy couple's wake.

197 Mix 'n' match

Let the official photographer do their job and take the all-important commissioned stills. Grab a few shots of the picture-taking, guests' reactions, confetti throwing, and the happy couple's departure.

198 Speeches

When it comes to recording speeches, you should find a position that will allow the viewer to see the speaker, as well as enough of the audience to see, as well as hear, their reaction.

199 Place your microphone

Think about how close you need to be for your microphone (built-in to the camcorder, or external, if you're using it) to pick up the speeches. Not all speakers project their voices well. With some non-directional mics you may record the conversation of the people around you, so make sure they're being polite!

200 Knowing when to stop

Many professional wedding videomakers capture the couple's first dance and the first few tunes from the band or disco. After that it can degenerate into drunken relative dancing! So that's up to you.

PARTIES AND EVENTS

201 Be prepared

Birthday parties, anniversaries, bachelor parties, etc, don't really allow the videomaker a chance to prepare. So be alert to capturing quick, funny, dramatic, or emotional moments.

202 Get talking

Get people talking. Try thinking of a few opening questions (what, why, how, when, where) to ask revellers, and they might tell you a few tales about the birthday boy or girl. It might be staged but at least you'll get personal reactions to treasure.

203 Add illumination

Indoor locations for events—especially if a band or disco is involved—can mean very low-light conditions. You could try using a video light to liven up the gloom, and get some better-looking shots.

204 Get in close

When light is low, get in close to the action. This way, the camcorder will at least pick up partygoers' faces. Long and medium shots will tend to fade to gray or look very grainy.

MUSIC VIDEOS AND PERFORMANCES

205 Advance planning

Again, planning is the key to success. Visit the venue prior to recording and work out where the best position for your camcorder or camcorders will be.

206 Use two camcorders

For recording concerts, two camcorders is the very least you should use, so ensure you get another camera operator involved. That way you can edit a dynamic video together.

207 Get the long shots

On a two-camcorder shoot, one operator should always be recording long shots. This way, you'll capture everything that happens on stage.

208 Close in on details

The second camcorder can be used to record medium and close-up shots. For example, you can capture a guitar solo or get audience reaction shots.

209 Record the whole song

Songs have beginnings and endings, so make sure you record from the start to the completion of a song. If you can, get to know the material of your chosen artist.

210 Recording sound

Sound recording is important (and tricky). Your options are varied.

- Record the whole song on the camcorder shooting long shots (Camera 1), and use that soundtrack, while you intercut between shots from Camera 1 and the camcorder recording close-ups (Camera 2).

- Cut between the sounds recorded on Camera 1 and Camera 2. This is not advised, though, as the volume levels will be different and will involve more work at the editing stage.

- Request the use of the live recording from the sound desk used at the event. This will provide a clean, consistent audio track. You could even ask for an audio cable to go from the sound desk directly into Camera 1.

211 Recording images

Most concert events use stage lighting. Make sure your camcorder can record images clearly. If necessary, use video lights.

212 Making a music video

If you want to record a music video, you should first work out a concept or theme with the artist. This can be a lot of fun for you both.

213 Select a location

Choose a location (or locations) that you know is safe and OK to use. Talk to local authorities and organizations. They can provide legal help and be on hand to clear up problems.

214 Storyboard your ideas

Use storyboards—simple sketches showing the action that is to take place—to show everyone involved what should be happening in each scene.

215 Use a music player

Use a portable music player so that you can play the song out loud. This is vital if your artist has to sing or mime along to their own recording.

DOCUMENTARY MAKING

216 Find your star

Documentary videomaking is a rewarding project for a novice. There are countless stories to be told: wildlife, environmental, political, social commentary, life history, and so on. Find a spokesperson who can really give a face and an original voice to an issue they are passionate about. Make the subject entertaining.

217 Be open to change

Be prepared for your story to change as you film. With most documentaries, there are always unexpected events. For instance, what happens when a local school is faced with closure?

218 Research your story

Research your topic thoroughly. Find out who all the key characters and organizations are, and contact them to find out if they'll talk to you. And if they won't, ask why.

219 Preparatory interviews

Conduct research interviews. Take your camcorder along whenever you visit a location or speak to someone. You might not use the footage, but you can use the information.

220 Stay chilled

Documentaries rarely offer the chance to reshoot, so learn to go with the flow of what's happening.

221 Do long takes

Unlike virtually all other types of videomaking, record long takes. This is because if you don't know what's going to happen, you can guarantee the exciting stuff will kick off when you've stopped recording.

222 Be bold

Use the editing process to chop out all the unnecessary material from your video.

223 Handhold

Tripods can limit your ability to move around when shooting a documentary. Go handheld with the camcorder to follow the action. Audiences are used to less smooth footage with this type of video.

RECORDING A VIDEO DIARY

224 Make it personal

A video diary is a great way of documenting a particular project, for example—following a diet or embarking on a training regime. It will be a record of a key moment in your life, and perhaps inspiring to others.

225 Feelings and images

You can also use a video diary as you would a paper diary. It's a way of recording feelings and emotions—this may be useful in years to come, or it may be something you prefer to erase!

226 The simple life

Best of all, a video diary doesn't require any fancy shooting techniques. You can just set the camcorder up so that you can see yourself on the LCD screen and talk away.

227 Frequent and honest

A video diary works best if you can be honest with yourself and, like a normal diary, if you make regular entries.

CAPTURING SPORTS ACTION

228 Action stations

Choosing to record a sporting event is a popular videomaking occasion. There is a wide range of subjects to pick from and, because there's always action involved, you're guaranteed to get some great recording opportunities.

229 Kids' sports

You might want to record a school sports event as a document of your children's sporting prowess. Remember to check with the school in advance that this is OK.

230 Call it a day

A day out at a Grand Prix or a horse racing meet is a fantastic chance to capture fast-moving action in atmospheric surroundings.

231 Team effort

If you're a member of a football, baseball, or hockey team, then you can help to video games. These can then be used to help improve performance, by showing your teammates what they're doing right and wrong.

232 Team tactics

You might also want to video your opponents before you play them, getting your colleagues some invaluable insights into how they might approach the game.

233 Self-improvement

Videos can help in individual sports, too. Cyclists, boxers, golfers, and tennis players can develop their performances by looking at improving a serve or a swing, or at which stages of an event they lose drive or impetus.

234 Smooth operater

Because fast-moving action can be just that—fast—use a tripod to make sure your footage is as smooth as possible. And practice any fast pans or tilts in advance.

235 Expect the unexpected

Follow the action as smoothly as possible from beginning to end. You're not always sure how events might unfold, so be on the lookout to capture as much as possible.

236 Leave plenty of room

Remember that phrase Lead Room? It's vital with sports that you leave enough space in front of the action for your subject to move into to "tell the story" to the viewer.

237 Put it into context

Use long shots to establish your location. The audience needs to know where you are and what they are meant to be watching before they can appreciate the onscreen action.

238 Get on down

A variety of angles will mean your footage will look as exciting as the action you're recording. Get down low when a car or bike whizzes past. It will seem so much faster.

239 On autopilot

In many cases, you can use the camcorder's auto settings, as this means you won't have to waste time setting focus and exposure.

240 Manual for close-ups

However, manual focus and exposure settings are invaluable when it's essential to get good close-ups. Practice and set up the manual focus and exposure modes in advance of shooting.

241 Blur can be good

Sometimes, blurred footage is actually a great video effect. Don't fear trailing or slightly out of focus shots if they add drama or tension.

242 Higher shutter speeds

Higher shutter speeds capture fast-moving action more smoothly. So if your camcorder has them, try using them.

243 Don't cross the line!

Make use of that Crossing the Line term you learned earlier. Shooting a car race and breaking that 180° rule, will leave your audience confused as to which direction the traffic's headed in!

MAKING A FICTION FILM

244 Breaking the rules

The great thing about making your own short or feature film, is that you're in control—and can break as many "rules" of videomaking as you like... as long as it works out.

245 A blank canvas

Subject-wise you have a blank canvas. That's both a boon and a problem: your story needs structure, dialog, and characters!

246 Plan your scenes

The ideal way to plan your movie is to make a visual storyboard of all the individual scenes, or make detailed notes on what you want each scene to contain. This will help you to make sense of your story as well as plan the shooting schedule.

247 Recruit your friends and family

You can keep costs low by getting family and friends involved, but make sure everyone's precisely briefed on what to do. And, if you can't pay them, at least feed them occasionally!

248 Hire, don't buy

Hire equipment when you think it's absolutely necessary. Lighting can be hired for a few days at a time. It'll cost much less than buying them outright.

249 Rehearse those lines

Get your actors to rehearse together as often as you can. It's no good knowing lines in isolation. Your cast needs to see how the whole piece fits together.

250 Learn from others

Watch lots of movies and TV shows. You'll pick up tips and clues in the most unlikely places. Wildlife documentaries are great for inventive camera angles.

Things to Make and Do

So, you know the technology, you've mastered the basics of composition, lighting, and sound recording, and learned how to apply them to any number of events, but there are still plenty more things to do. After all those rules and guidelines, it's time to have a little more fun with the camcorders. In this section we'll give you little tips that will make shooting easier, teach you how to carry out some of the special shots you've seen at the movies, and tell you how to make your own special effects and accessories that won't break the bank.

SUGAR GLASS

251 Give me some sugar!

Sugar glass, or breakaway glass, is one of those special effects that you constantly see on television and at the movies. Every time someone dives through a window or gets hit with a bottle, sugar glass is used instead of the real thing. People tend to assume that it's an expensive special effect but, in fact, it costs very little and is easy to make.

252 What's cooking?

The ingredients for sugar glass are just simple items you can get in the supermarket and from the tap. You need two parts water, one part corn syrup, and three-and-a-half parts sugar.

253 Kitchenware

A thermometer, and a pan big enough to hold the amount of mix you want to make, are the most important tools. You will also need a non-stick tray to set your sugar glass in, or a mold if you're going to shape it into a bottle or a vase.

254 On the boil

First things first, mix all your ingredients together in a warm pan and slowly bring it to the boil. The boiling point of the mixture will depend on the quality of the sugar and syrup you've used, but knowing the temperature will be important. Once the mix is boiling, take the temperature with a thermometer and make a note of it.

255 Steady as she goes

Once the mixture is boiling, keep it at that temperature for about 15 minutes to cook properly.

256 Seasoning

At this point, you might want to add a small pinch of salt to the mixture. It's not vital that you do so, but the salt will take some of the shine off the finished glass. If you're molding a fake window you probably want the shine, but bottle glass tends to be a little duller, so the salt is handy when you're making that sort of prop.

257 Crank it up

Once the mixture has had about 15 minutes on the boil, you need to raise the temperature to boil off some of the excess water. You need to bring the temperature up by 50°F from boiling point. So, if your mixture hit boiling at 100°F, for example, you need to crank the heat up to 150°F.

258 Sounding good?

Once it hits the right temperature, dip the end of the thermometer into the mix then let a little of the mixture drip off the end into a pot of cold water. It should make a sound like breaking glass. Once your mixture hits 50°F above boiling or makes that sound, it's ready. Pour it into your mold or tray and leave it to cool and set.

259 Use-by date

Sugar glass doesn't last that long once it's set before it begins to warp out of shape or get sticky. Ideally, it's best to schedule any shots requiring sugar glass for an afternoon and make the glass first thing in the morning, rather than leaving it overnight.

260 Safety first

The advantages of sugar glass are that it's far more brittle than real glass, not as hard, and rarely takes on a sharp edge when it breaks. That said, it's still worth being careful. If you're going to jump through it, try to wear thick resilient clothing. Better yet, use a spring-loaded hammer or mousetrap to shatter the glass a split second before you hit it. It will still look as if you've jumped through it, but will be slightly safer. If possible, test a small piece of sugar glass from the same batch to see how it breaks, before using the main piece.

BULLET HITS

261 Open fire

Probably the most commonly attempted special effect is that of bullet hits. It seems that as soon as anyone picks up a camcorder they want to film an action scene. Actual cinema bullet hits usually involve pyrotechnic squibs, which are too dangerous to play around with at home. You can, however, make a blow gun that will allow you to create a similar effect.

262 Construction material

You'll need a 16 inch (40.5cm) piece of aluminum tubing with a diameter of about $1/3$ inch (1cm), a microphone stand, eight inches (20.3cm) of stretchable rubber tubing, and a set of bellows to provide the "blow" for your blowgun. Do not used compressed air—professionals can get away with it, but you run the risk of hurting someone if you hit them with a compressed-air projectile.

263 Ingredients

You need two recipes for bullet hits—one is for fake blood, the other is for the effect of the hit itself. You will need a tin of processed peas, red food coloring, blue food coloring, corn syrup, and some milk or condensed milk.

264 Life blood

The first thing you need to mix is the fake blood. The actual amounts you need to mix depends very much on the color and consistency of the fake blood you want to produce. Your main ingredients are the corn syrup and red food coloring, which are mixed to create the base blood.

265 Dark matters

The base fake blood will be bright red and transparent. If you need it to be a little darker, add a few drops of the blue food coloring. In order to make the blood slightly more opaque, like real blood, add a small amount of milk or condensed milk. For use with the blow gun, use ordinary milk, as the condensed variety will only make an already sticky mixture even stickier.

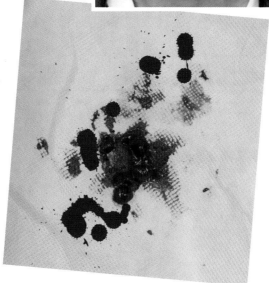

266 Hit-makers

Now for the bullet hits themselves. First, gently boil your processed peas to soften them slightly, then place them in a container and fill it with red food coloring. Leave them overnight to soak up as much of the redness as possible. Then drain them and add your fake blood mixture to the container and let them soak in that for a while.

267 Building the blow gun

Place the aluminum tube in the head of the mic stand and adjust it to the correct height for your target. Place one end of the rubber tubing over the end of the aluminum tube and the other over the end of the fireplace bellows. Give them a test squeeze. If the pressure is enough to pop the rubber tube off either end, then secure it with a cable tie.

268 The fun part

Now you're ready to go. Load one of your sloppy red peas into the blow gun, aim it at your target from just out of shot, run the cameras... aim... fire!

SETS AND PROPS

269 Dressing up

Sometimes, the real world just isn't interesting enough for your movies, and you'll need to dress a set with very odd or very specific furnishings. This doesn't have to mean breaking the bank by purchasing the props you need.

270 Foam party

Blue foam is the disposable design material of choice. Search the Internet, or visit your local crafts or modeling store for blue foam to find a supplier.

271 Working with foam

Blue foam is a thick, bright blue substance with a texture somewhere between stryrofoam and sponge. It can be cut with a stanley knife, saw, or hot wire, shaped with a plane or harsh sandpaper, and smoothed with a smooth sandpaper. You can create pretty much any shape you desire from it, and although it's not particularly durable, it can be painted to look like anything you want.

272 Precautions

Shaping blue foam takes time, as you'll usually be taking a large block and working it down slowly into the object you need, piece by piece. It's messy stuff that produces a large amount of blue dust as it's cut or sanded. If possible, shape your blue foam in a garage or outdoors, and wear a cloth mask over your mouth and nose, and goggles. Although not actually dangerous, the particles produced are small, and very irritating if inhaled.

Restaurants and other similar public spaces may be prepared to allow you to film while they are closed. The advantages of not having to deal with spectators as well as the actors and crew are clear.

REFLECTORS

273 Maintaining a reflection

Reflectors are the simplest way of redirecting natural or artificial light to where you want it, as well as adding some color along the way. Properly manufactured reflectors are best, but they're a waste of money if you'll only use them very occasionally. Homemade reflectors can be constructed easily on the cheap.

276 Be direct

For very direct reflections, coat a piece of foamboard in tinfoil. The foil is highly reflective and allows you to cast a harsh and tight reflection, ideal for adding highlights to a scene. Because aluminum has a shiny and dull side you can vary the intensity of the reflection.

274 Card tricks

The easiest homemade reflector is a piece of white foamboard, also known as foam core. This is a stiff piece of foam sandwiched between two laminated pieces of white card, and can be bought in any art supply store. Cut it into a usable size using a craft knife—you're likely to need it either two feet by four feet (0.6 by 1.2m), or four feet by six feet (1.2 by 1.8m), depending on the light source you intend to reflect.

277 Foiled again

To avoid wrinkling the foil, which will scatter the light, try to cut the foil to size first on a flat surface, then attach double-sided sticky tape, then place the card on top of it. Alternatively, if you want a very scattered look to the light, wrinkle the foil a lot, stretch it out flat again, the attach it to your card.

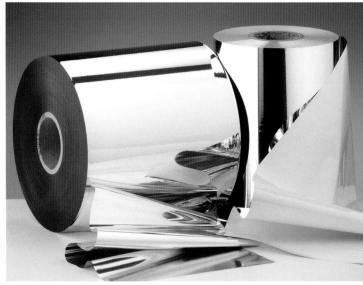

275 Scattering the light

The laminated white of the foamboard reflects your light source quite strongly, and might not be suitable for your shot. To make the light less harsh, take a thin white bed sheet and wrap it twice around the board, then hold it in place with staples on the reverse. This will reflect the light but in a softer, more diffuse manner.

278 Warmth from cold metal

Don't just stick to ordinary silver-colored catering foil. Experimenting with different colors can benefit your films. Although colored foil will reduce the amount of light reflected slightly, it more than makes up for it in effect. Gold foil, for example, will give a warm, sunshine glow, great for bringing out the best in pale-skinned people.

279 Back on track

One of the most bravura moves in filmmaking is the extended tracking shot. You've seen it plenty of times—the camera constantly moving along as it follows the action slowly. Sadly, the dolly tracks or steadicam used to accomplish this are beyond the budget of most casual videomakers, but a reasonable substitute is available.

280 Bagging it

The trick with the tracking shot is to isolate the camera from the movement of your body in order to keep the shots smooth. This can be accomplished by customizing an old gym bag. First, cut a slot in one end for the lens, then cut away the top of the bag so that you can see the camcorder screen. Position the cam in the bag with the screen pointing up at you and tape it securely. Next, tape a few small weights into the bag so that it will hang properly from its handles.

281 Tread carefully

With the bag held outwards, away from the movement of your body, hanging from its handles in your hand, you can walk around slowly, following the action, with most of your movement absorbed by the bag handles.

HOMEMADE DOLLY ZOOMS

282 Wheely good ideas

Of course, you can carry out dolly shots using just about anything with wheels. The lack of tracks limits you to smooth terrain only, but there are still plenty of times when a homemade dolly will come in handy. The most common substitute dolly is a wheelchair. Sit your camera operator in it and push. We've seen just about everything used as a substitute dolly, from shopping carts to skateboards, depending on the height that's needed.

283 The dolly zoom

As soon as people have a dolly, they want to do a dolly zoom. This is the unsettling effect used in Hitchcock's *Vertigo* and Spielberg's *Jaws*, in which the background seems to move, looming up behind a stationery subject in the foreground.

284 How it works

Variously known as the contrazoom, trombone shot, or occasionally the zolly, dolly zooms take advantage of the way that a zoom lens brings the background closer, not by moving the lens but by compressing the middle ground. This has the effect of altering perspective without changing the subject size–completely the opposite of what the human eye expects to see.

285 Experimental shots

The procedure for a dolly zoom is acually quite simple, but the timing is difficult to get right as the speeds of the dolly and the zoom need to be fairly close to each other. Place a subject within a few feet of your lens, with an interesting background some distance away. Trees or buildings work better than a flat landscape. Using your wheelchair dolly, move backward slowly, away from your subject, while zooming in at a speed relative to the backward movement. Although the effect is noticeable in the movement of the background, the trick is to concentrate on your foreground subject, keeping them the right size in the frame.

286 Physical panning

If you haven't got a tripod it can be difficult to carry out panning shots smoothly by hand, but it's not impossible. In the same way that there are physical techniques for lifting heavy objects, there are physical techniques for panning, too.

287 Start at the end

In order to pan smoothly without a tripod, you need to move your body in certain ways. Start by facing where you want the pan to end. Position yourself in a comfortable, natural shooting position and anchor your feet.

288 Set up the start

Now have the action set up and ready to go at the point where the pan will start following it from. Put the camcorder to your eye and carefully twist yourself backwards from the waist into position to start the pan, while leaving your feet placed exactly as they were.

289 Action...

Just before the action starts, slightly bend your knees and slowly unwind your body to pan along with what you're shooting.

290 ... and pan!

By loading all the pressure onto your muscles from the start and unwinding to a comfortable position, you'll accomplish a much smoother pan.

291 Problematic panning

With DVD and solid-state camcorders that compress your video into MPEG on the fly, pans can be a problem, as the compression works by recognizing the movement in the shot. By moving the whole camcorder, you give it a lot of work to do. Try to keep it slow and gentle.

AVOIDING THE SHAKES

292 Walk like an Egyptian

When walking with a camcorder you need to make a bit of a fool of yourself in order to keep the shot smooth. The idea is to turn your body into a shock absorber whilst adjusting your gait to produce minimal movement.

293 Crouching cameraman, hidden movement

First you need to curl your body into a slight crouch in an attempt to centralize your weight and soften your motion. Then bend your knees slightly and try to keep them bent as the flex will soak up some of your footfalls.

294 On the move

As you walk, lengthen your stride slightly—not enough to lurch, but enough that each step becomes very careful and deliberate. Place one foot in front of the other as if walking along a beam, to minimize side-to-side motion.

295 Hold your breath

Although impossible for long walks with the camcorder, on short walks it's worth trying to hold your breath. Inhalations expand your chest and lift your shoulders, taking the camcorder with it. The exhale then reverses the effect.

296 Assume the position

When shooting from a stationary position, keep your elbows tucked in to your body as close as you can to keep the camera stable. Better yet, rest your elbows on something solid.

297 Zoom focus

When preparing a shot, zoom your camcorder in slightly before you adjust the focus. Once you've got the image sharp, zoom back out to the original position—the image will only get sharper. This is a trick used by professional camera operators all the time, and is equally useful on basic camcorders.

298 Softening focus

Alternatively, you may want a softer focus with a defined area on it. For example, fogging the surroundings of a shot while leaving part of it clear. This can be accomplished by attaching a skylight filter to the lens then smearing it lightly with Vaseline. This is ideal for focus effects where you can't depend on simply adjusting depth of field.

300 Crystal blacking

Crystal blacking allows for smoother recording and editing by laying down a continuous timecode on your DV tape. Prior to recording, completely block all light from your lens, then record the length of the tape. Then rewind the tape ready for use—the new data path when you actually carry out the proper shoot will run more smoothly onto the tape.

299 Softening skin

The years aren't always kind to some people, and you might want to take away a few blemishes and wrinkles from your subject. Many camcorders have a "soft skin" mode for doing this, but it can also be accomplished by stretching a pair of thin nylon pantyhose over the lens.

Video Editing

Editing your work

In this section, you'll learn how to edit your videos. We'll guide you through the equipment, the creative skills you need to learn, and even teach you the basic procedures for using four of the most commonplace video editing programs on the market—two of which are free! If you can edit your videos, then you can make sure no one ever gets bored of your vacation films by removing all the dull stuff, you can caption birthday parties, and add titles to school plays. And if you're making a fiction movie, you can create timing and tension in the same way that Hollywood does. In fact, we'd go so far as to say that in most cases an unedited video is an unfinished video.

BUYING A COMPUTER

One of the reasons for the popularity of digital video is the fact that the video information is already in a language that a computer can understand, making it very easy to transfer your footage from camcorder to computer and edit it, add special effects and titles, and then put the finished product back on tape, DVD, or the Internet. You don't have to do all that if you don't want to, but having a good computer to partner your camcorder opens up a world of possibilities.

301 Apple Macs

The first choice you'll have to make when buying a computer is to decide which operating system you want to use. Apple Macintosh computers are very popular with video editors because they're stable and stylish, and, because the basic hardware and software packages are all made by the same company, they tend to work straight from the box. On the other hand, Macs tend to be slightly more expensive than Windows PCs and are less of a priority for software developers. Macs come equipped with an entry-level video editing program called iMovie, which will get you started on video editing, and there are more advanced Mac-based packages, such as Final Cut.

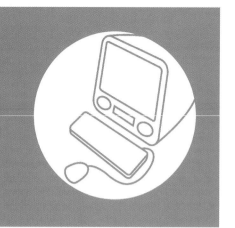

302 Windows PC

Microsoft's Windows is by far and away the most common operating system in the world and, as such, benefits from the fact that pretty much everyone is familiar with it, knows how to work it, and can provide an informal web of help and support to the less technologically minded. Windows also benefits from its ubiquity by being a priority for most software developers, giving you a world of choice. Like a Mac, a Windows PC comes with an entry-level video editing program called Windows MovieMaker.

303 Linux

If you're more technologically minded and willing to break from the norm, it may be worth considering running Linux. This is an "open source" operating system, meaning that the core "kernel" of code that goes into the operating system is available to everyone to play with and modify (as opposed to being a copyrighted thing, like Windows). This means that pretty much anyone with an open source operating system is able to write programs, fix problems, and come up with handy little software tools, which are then shared among other users like a great big adventure in communal computing. Linux machines are probably the most stable systems available, but they do represent a steep learning curve for new users.

304 FireWire

FireWire goes under a variety of names depending on which manufacturer is supplying it, from IEEE1394 to i.Link. Essentially, FireWire is a cable-and-socket system that enables extremely fast data transfer and device control. This is important, because digital video contains a lot of information, so a fast system helps speed the transfer of that information from camcorder to computer, and the device control aspect allows you to operate your camcorder via your computer. Most computers now have a FireWire or FireWire 800 (a faster version of the same thing) connection. If the model you're looking at doesn't have FireWire, buy a different one if you're serious about video.

305 RAM

RAM is Random Access Memory, essentially the short-term memory that your computer uses to hold any information it is actively working with, such as a video editing program and the video files that are being edited. The more RAM you have, the more information your computer can work with at any given time. Once again, the size of video files makes this an important factor. As a minimum, we'd suggest getting a computer with at least 512MB (Megabytes) of RAM. Already video is progressing, with new types of High Definition (HD) video demanding at least 1GB (Gigabyte) of RAM. You don't necessarily need to worry about this immediately, as you might never need that much RAM, and if you do it's very easy to buy and fit more RAM to a computer. Make sure your computer has at least a couple of empty slots in which you can fit extra DIMMs (RAM modules) if you need them.

306 Bits and bytes

Digital information is measured in bits and bytes. Bits are the smallest piece of computer information—there are eight bits to a byte, 1,024 bytes to a kilobyte, and so on. Manufacturers often round this figure down to 1,000 for easy arithmetic, which means that often a product doesn't have quite the capacity you think it does—a 40GB hard disk drive, for example, is usually more like 39.5GB.

307 Processors

The processor is the brain of your computer. Essentially, a processor breaks any task you give it down into millions of simple questions with a yes or no answer, then does all the calculations involved in getting those answers before reassembling all the information as a completed task. When you see a processor claiming to be 700MHz (Megahertz) what it is saying is that it can perform 700 million calculations per second. The speed of your processor directly relates to your computer's ability to do a job—the faster it can think, the faster you can work. If your processor isn't fast enough to carry out the work a piece of software gives it, then that software won't work, so a fast processor is very important.

308 Internal hard disk

If RAM is your computer's short-term memory, then the hard disk is its long-term memory, where all the software, files, and documents are stored when not in use. Hard disk capacities are measured in gigabytes. Given that 20 minutes of digital video takes up about four gigabytes, you can see that it's important to have a very large hard disk drive to store your work.

309 External hard disk

You might want to consider getting an external hard disk that plugs into the FireWire socket of your computer. This isn't essential, but it will allow you to store all your video files in one place without cluttering up your computer's internal hard drive, which will fill up very quickly once you start working with video. If you do buy an external hard drive, look for one with a fast connection, ideally FireWire, and a high speed (at least 7,200RPM) as this will allow it to transfer video data to your computer as fast as your computer needs it. If the drive can't keep up with demand, you will suffer dropped frames (bits of video going missing.)

310 Minimum requirements

Most software has on its box a minimum system requirements list, which will tell you how much RAM is needed, how fast the processor should be, and how much hard disk space is required for the software. Take these requirements seriously—if your computer doesn't meet them, then the software might not work. Even if it does, if you only just meet the system requirements, you might find that certain features are unavailable or work slowly and unreliably. The higher the specifications of your machine, the better the software will work.

311 Upgrading

Almost all desktop computers and, to a lesser extent, laptops, give you some options for upgrading the machine to a better specification. Usually you will find a couple of empty slots for DIMMs, which are printed circuit boards with extra RAM on them, and an empty bay or two into which you can place extra hard disk drives, or DVD writers. You will also find that whatever operating system you use (Mac, Windows, Linux, etc) evolves regularly, with tweaks and changes made. Most of these tweaks come in the form of free downloads from the manufacturer, but every few years or so manufacturers will do a massive overhaul of the operating system that will most likely cost you a small upgrade fee. All this means that if your computer isn't ideally specced to start with, you can improve it bit by bit as and when you have the money. Basic upgrades such as fitting more RAM or adding a drive are very easy to carry out and nothing to be afraid of.

EDITING PRINCIPLES

So, you've got your footage on tape in your camcorder, you've got your swanky computer, and you're ready to start editing. The next set of tips will tell you how to prepare for the edit and what sort of cuts and joins you can make.

312 Be constructive

People often focus their attention on the destructive part of editing, simply working out which shots are extraneous and hacking them out. Try to think constructively—editing is as much about how you join up the footage you want as it is about removing the footage you don't.

313 Visualization

Before you start shooting, try drawing a storyboard that shows all your camera angles and how one shot joins to the next. This will save you hours of time in the editing room by giving you a blueprint for your edit, and will also save on wasted tape by making sure you know in advance what you do and don't need to shoot.

314 Cutting room

You should be thinking about the edit while you're still shooting. When you get to the end of a shot, hold it for a few seconds longer than you'll eventually need it to be. This will give you room to make the cut when the time comes.

315 Logging

If your movie is going to contain more information than your storage medium (disk, tape, card) can hold, keep a log that contains details of every take of every shot, along with its timecode location (if appropriate) and any comments about quality.

316 Get coverage

Coverage is the professional term for getting all the shots that an editor might need to work with. It doesn't mean shooting everything in sight, but it does mean making sure they have shots that identify the location and the participants, known as establishing shots, as well as those containing all the action.

317 Masters & cutaways

As well as establishing shots it's also a good idea to get a master shot and some cutaways. The master is a wide shot of the whole scene in a single take, and cutaways are various close-ups on items or people in the scene. If you have these then you can assemble a workable version of the scene should anything go wrong with the more complicated version you storyboard. That's why master shots are sometimes called safety shots. They're insurance.

318 Timeline editors

There are two main types of video editing software. The first is the timeline style. In this, all your video and audio is placed on specific tracks you create for them, and the length of each shot is represented by the length of the shot icon on the timeline. The advantage of timelines is that they make it easy to see how your project fits together and to do cutaways. The uppermost element on a timeline is what plays, so a two second clip placed on a timeline track above and halfway along a 10 second clip will mean that you'll automatically cut from the 10 second clip to the two second one and back again.

319 Storyboard editors

Better suited to beginners are storyboard-editing layouts, in which all the clips are represented by a single icon and shown in sequence. A storyboard simply shows shot one next to shot two, and so on. You can then rearrange shots by dragging them into different orders.

320 One window or two?

The other common distinguishing factor in video editing software is the choice of a single- or double-window layout. A two-window layout has one window that will play back any video dropped into it from the storage bin, while the other plays back what's on the timeline. This means you can use the first window for trimming clips and creating effects, and the other to keep a general overview of your project. Single windows combine both tools into a single monitor window.

321 In the bin

Bins are where you keep all the files associated with your video. They are displayed onscreen in your video editing software and help you keep yourself organized by creating a filing system. For example, we usually have a bin for video clips, another for audio clips, a third for effects, and another for titles. You can find the arrangement that suits you, but do try to use the bins, as they break complicated projects down into easy-to-handle chunks.

322 Cut for meaning, then for feel

This is a maxim used by professional editors and it means exactly what it says. When you first cut together a scene, concentrate on making sure it says everything it has to say, then work on adding the shots that get across the feelings it should convey. For example, a scene with lots of people shouting and looking angry will convey the feelings, but not the crux of the conflict in the scene. You need to get the argument assembled coherently before your audience can make sense of the characters' behavior.

323 Context

Pudovkin and Kuleshov, two Russian editors working in the 1920s, discovered that the same shot of a man's face was interpreted differently by audiences depending on what was shown before or after it. Using shots of a child, a bowl of soup, and a coffin, the same image of the face was made to convey parental pride, hunger, and grief. Keep this in mind when editing—you make the shots convey whatever you want them to by linking them to other shots. On their own they can be anything, in your hands they can be what you want them to be.

324 Continuity editing

There are three main styles of editing. Continuity is the most common, and its purpose is to truncate real time into screen time without the audience noticing that anything has been edited. For example, a man may take five minutes to make a cup of coffee, but careful editing of a kettle being filled, coffee being spooned into a cup, the kettle spout whistling, water being poured, and the man drinking can turn those five minutes into 30 seconds, without spoiling the audience's illusions.

325 Parallel editing

Parallel editing is useful for building tension in your audience. Say, for example, you have two separate sequences such as a groom arriving at a church and a bride getting ready for the big day. They may have taken place at different times, but if you cut back and forth from one to the other you both truncate the time and relate the two sequences to each other, allowing your audience to get excited about how one sequence affects the other. You still need to arrange the shots in the same order as you would with continuity editing, but you also cut between the two sequences at regular intervals.

326 Montage editing

Sometimes referred to as collision editing, montage editing states that two seemingly unrelated shots, known as thesis and antithesis, can be combined to make clear something that is apparent in neither of them: synthesis. For example, someone in a bright office working frantically, followed by the same person slumped in a dark bar looking drunk, will combine to suggest the sort of toll hard work is taking on the character.

327 Motivation

When cutting from one shot to another, try to find motivation— a reason to cut from one shot to the next. It could be a noise offscreen, a movement onscreen, even a simple flicker in a character's eyeline. Having something trigger or motivate a cut makes your editing feel more seamless.

328 Hold it right there!

Think about how long you need to hold a shot onscreen for in order for your audience to make sense of it. Something likely to be familiar to your audience, such as a simple house on a street, needs much less time onscreen than, say, an ornate palace.

Here's a logical sequence of edits: at the beginning of the scene, our two protagonists are seen together in a medium two-shot; next, the camera zooms in to focus on their conversation; last, is the reaction shot from a third character—in this movie, the antagonist.

In this in-depth chapter on video editing, you'll learn the skills you need to transform your basic shots into a slickly edited package, including titles and effects, which you can then burn onto a DVD, complete with professional-looking menu.

329 | Move it

If you're cutting on a movement, you run the risk of accidentally creating a jump cut that will jar your audience and break the spell. Try to match the rates of movement and the relative size of objects between one cut and the next for a smoother transition.

330 | Using inserts

Inserts or cutaways are very short shots dropped into longer ones for the purpose of clarification and variety. If someone talks about a vase, adding an insert of the vase focuses the audience's attention and provides a break from the original shot.

331 | Take 'em to the bridge

Inserts can also be used when a piece of footage is mostly OK but maybe has one or two bad moments such as a camera wobble or loss of focus. By leaving the audio intact but cutting away to a relevant insert at the bad moment, you can cover a multitude of sins and save otherwise good footage.

VIDEO EDITING

Getting rid of unnecessary footage (mistakes, boring moments, and footage that just doesn't look good) helps to make a better-looking movie. You'll get more satisfaction watching it, and so will your friends. But trimming clips isn't the only aspect of editing. You can add titles and also effects, such as dissolves and crossfades, so clips flow seamlessly into one another. You can even include a new soundtrack, with music or narration. Editing might seem like a complex subject but it's not. It's just a whole new range of things you can do to make better home movies. Here we're going to look at some editing software programs for your home computer. You'll find there's software to suit every budget and ability.

Over the next few chapters we'll teach you the basics of editing with four different programs. iMovie (Mac) and MovieMaker (Windows) are designed for beginners, and are provided free with most computers and are therefore most likely to be the first editing programs you encounter, while the different versions of Final Cut and Adobe Premiere are the common choices for more ambitious editors on Mac and PC respectively.

IMOVIE

Apple's iMovie application comes bundled with all new/recent Apple Macs as part of the iLife suite that is included with the Mac operating system, which includes applications such as iPhoto, iTunes, and iDVD. For those with slightly earlier OS X Macs, you can purchase iLife as a shrinkwrapped bundle. With the latest Macs being positioned as remote-controlled digital entertainment and creativity centers, it's a powerful set of tools by any standard.

332 | What is iMovie?

iMovie is Apple's entry level, non-linear editing software. It gives you a range of basic tools for editing your movies, together with some fun special effects and atmospheres that you can use to add drama to your existing shots–e.g. lightning flashes, a snowstorm, and "old movie" textures.

333 What can it do?

iMovie provides the basic tools for capturing video from your camcorder into your computer, cutting it to length, reordering it, adding special effects, titles, and soundtracks, and exporting it back to tape, onto DVD, onto the Internet, or even to a video-equipped cellphone.

334 Why do we like it?

iMovie is designed for beginners and is incredibly easy to use, yet it's still capable of producing results of a very high standard. Films made using iMovie have even made it into movie theaters and the Cannes Film Festival. Furthermore, because iMovie is well integrated with the rest of iLife, it makes it very easy to use stills and audio from iPhoto and iTunes within your video, and export projects to iDVD.

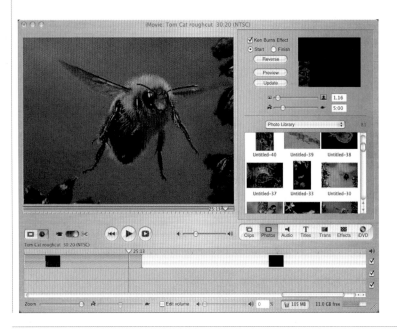

335 Window display

The first thing you need to be aware of in iMovie is the display window. This is where you watch the video that you're working with. It can be used to play clips from the bin or the timeline, and the little handles on the timeline built into the display window can be dragged to where you want a particular clip to begin and end, making it easy to trim video clips to the size you want.

336 Timeline

iMovie's timeline displays your video and audio channels, and the length of the clips you have on them, giving your project a jigsaw-like appearance. Using the timeline you can see how different pieces of footage fit together. If that's too complicated, the timeline can be turned into a storyboard that shows a simpler linear progression of clips.

337 In the bin

The bin varies according to what icon is selected on the menu palette, and shows all the relevant files for the selected icon. In clip mode it shows all the video clips you've captured; in audio mode it shows all the tunes in your audio library; in transitions mode it shows the various transitions you can apply to your footage. To incorporate files from the bin into your video, drag them from the bin onto the timeline.

338 The Menu palette

The Menu palette is displayed beneath the bin and is used to select files that are shown in the bin. When you click the icon on the palette that relates to something customizable, such as a transition, it will change the bin to display the controls used to customize the transition, as well as showing you all the transitions that are available.

339 Capturing video

Plug your camcorder's FireWire output into your computer's FireWire socket, then click the toggle beneath the display window so that it moves from the scissors icon to the camera icon. iMovie can now control your camcorder.

340 Importing video

Use the Play button onscreen to play through the tape in your camcorder. When the piece of video you want to capture starts to run on the screen, click the Import button and iMovie will bring that video into the clip bin—when you reach the end of the clip, hit the Import button again to stop the procedure. Carry on doing this until all the clips you want have been imported to the clip bin.

341 Putting video on the timeline

Click the toggle back from the camcorder to the scissors icon to enter iMovie's editing mode, then select the first clip you want to use by clicking and dragging it from the bin onto the timeline.

342 Viewing the timeline

Just above the timeline are two icons–a filmstrip and a clock. If you click the clock icon, your timeline will be displayed as differently sized chunks of separate video and audio. This view is good for fitting together intricate sequences and adjusting clip lengths. The little arrow with the line coming out of it is called the playhead–its position on the timeline indicates the location of what's shown in the display window.

343 Viewing the storyboard

If you click the filmstrip icon, the timeline turns into a storyboard–this displays only a sequence of icons representing the clips you've edited, but not their duration or audio tracks. This mode is handy for an overview, and for quickly adding transitions by simply dragging and dropping them between icons.

344 Trimming clips

Sometimes you need to shorten a clip. There are two ways to do this. The first is to click the end of the clip on the timeline and drag it to the left, until it's where you want it to end. To fine-tune this, use the left and right cursor keys to drag the clip back or forward one frame at a time. Alternatively, you can click on the blue bar at the bottom of the display window and drag the two yellow arrows inwards. This lets you trim the beginning and end of the clip to specific lengths, useful if you only want the middle piece of the clip.

345 Restore, duplicate, and paste

Trimming the clip doesn't mean you can't also use it at full length elsewhere on your timeline. You can drag the clip back to full length by reversing what you did in Tip 344. You can also copy the clip by clicking on it, then selecting Copy from the Edit menu. Next, you can paste the copy onto the timeline by moving the playhead to the point where you want to insert the video and selecting Paste from the Edit menu.

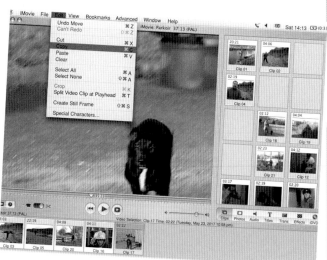

346 Creating titles

Having trimmed and assembled all your clips you can then add a title. Click the T icon in the Menu palette and select the font you want to use from the list. Then type the title you want into the boxes provided.

347 Adjust the title

Drag the slider back and forth between the big and little "A" until the text in the preview window is the size you want it to be in proportion to the rest of your video. Then click the box marked Color. A wheel will appear showing various colors in varying tones—click the part of the wheel that matches the color you want your title to be.

348 Style it up

Scroll through the list of text effects and choose a style that suits your video. By clicking an effect, you can see it previewed in the window at the top of the bin.

349 What a drag

Having chosen a font, size, color, and style, click the icon in the list and drag it down to the timeline. Once you've dropped it onto the timeline, a few moments will pass as iMovie prepares a preview which will let you see the text as part of your video project.

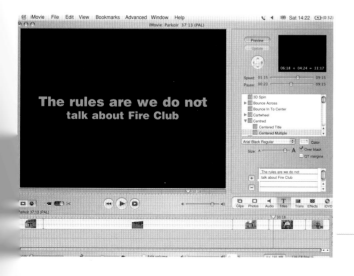

350 Playing with pictures

An advantage of iMovie is that it works with a photo management program called iPhoto and lets you add stills to your video. Click the photos icon in the Menu palette to display a list of all the photos in your iPhoto library. Click on a photo and adjust its display size and screen time duration by dragging the blue blob along the two sliders above the list.

351 The Burns' effect

The Ken Burns' effect, named for the man who used it so effectively in the PBS Civil War documentary, adds a bit of life to stills by panning across them or around them. It's a great way of compensating for the lack of motion in a still photo. The effect can be turned off by clicking the blue tickbox.

352 Adding a still to the timeline

Once you're happy with the photo you've chosen, click and drag it to the timeline the same way you dragged the text. If you've used the Ken Burns' effect there will be a slight delay as iMovie renders the photo.

353 Adding audio: Step 1

Now we're going to add music and narration to the video. The first step is to turn off the pre-existing audio so that it doesn't interfere with your fine-tuning of the new audio. At the end of the timeline, click the blue tickbox next to the audio track. When the box is gray and unticked, the audio track is still present, but won't play back.

354 Adding audio: Step 2

Click the audio icon to display the contents of your iTunes library, then click the song you want and hit the play button to listen to it.

355 Adding audio: Step 3

Drag the playhead along the timeline to the spot where you want the music to start, then hit the place at playhead button. There will be a slight delay while iMovie converts the song to a format it can use, then the music will appear in the audio channel that still has a tick in its box.

356 Adding narration

If you want to add narration, select the target audio track to record the narration by unclicking the tickbox on the other audio track, then plug a microphone into your computer's mic input, hit the red record button next to the microphone display in the audio bin, and begin speaking. When you're done, hit the record button again to stop recording. If you make a mistake, drag the playhead back to the beginning and repeat the process to record over the first attempt.

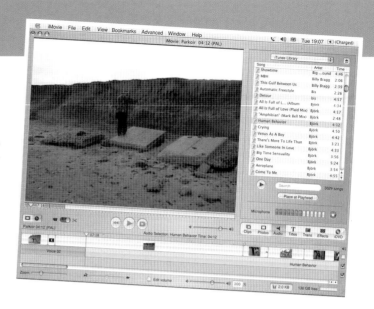

357 Adjusting audio levels

You can adjust the audio levels on-the-fly so that different sections of the same audio channel have different volumes. In the View menu, select Show Audio Waveforms and Show Clip Volume Levels. The waveform displays the peaks and troughs of the audio, while the black line in the middle is the volume. Drag the line up or down for an overall increase or decrease. Alternatively, click at two different spots on the line to make pegs appear—you can drag these pegs up and down, and the volume line between them will adjust to correspond. For example, to fade the audio down slowly, create the first peg where the fade will start, and the second where it will end, then drag the second peg downward to the level you want it to end at.

358 Selecting transitions

Transitions are changes from one clip to the next. A straight cut is a type of transition, but the ones that appear when you click the transitions icon are rather more stylized. Click on the transitions icon and scroll through the list until you find one that you like.

359 Adjust the duration

A transition with a duration of 10 seconds won't work if the clips on either side of it are shorter than 10 seconds, so you'll need to drag the blue blob on the speed slider to a length that fits between your two clips.

360 Add the transition

The easiest way to add your transition is to switch into the storyboard mode, as this displays the clips as simple icons. Drag your chosen transition from the menu and hover it over the icons and they'll slide apart to accommodate the transition. Release the mouse button to drop the transition into place.

361 iDVD integration

DVD is now the most common way to distribute home movies. We'll cover the full procedure later on, but in preparation for it, you can add chapter marks in your project now. Click the iDVD icon in the Menu palette, drag the playhead to the point where you want a chapter break to occur, then hit the add chapter button.

362 Saving your work

It's rare that you'll be able to edit and export an entire project in one go, so it's important to save your work as you go along. In the File menu, select Save As and give it a simple, recognizable title.

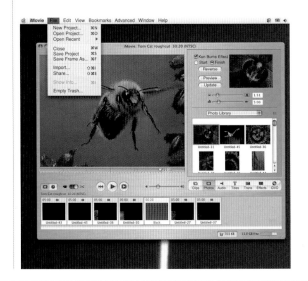

WINDOWS MOVIEMAKER

This software program is from Microsoft and has been designed for beginners. It has a simple layout (or interface as it's known) and is for a PC- not a Mac-user. The big advantage is that if you've got Windows XP, you've got it–it's already installed and ready to use, just waiting in the accessories folder under your Start button.

364 Step 2: Name your video clips

MovieMaker will prompt you to name your video clips, and ask if you want to capture the whole tape automatically, or bits of it manually.

363 Step 1: Capture video

As long as your computer has a FireWire port you can plug in a camcorder, and select Capture from Video Camera from the menu at the left of the screen.

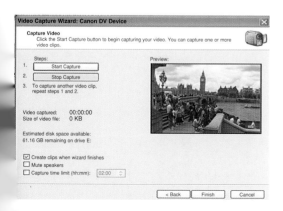

365 Step 3: Load additional footage

If you want to include footage you've captured previously, or already have on disk from another source, just select File/Import Into Collections and it will be loaded into the Collection window.

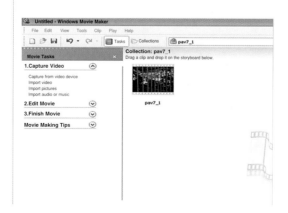

366 Step 4: Drop a clip onto the storyboard

Grab one of your shots from the Collections window and drag it into the first empty slot on the storyboard (at the bottom of the screen).

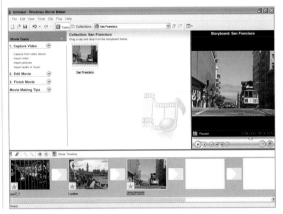

367 Step 5: Add another clip

Now drag in another shot next to it. This creates your first edit. Hit play (just below the monitor on the right hand side of the screen) and your two shots will play through.

368 Step 6: Change the order of clips

You can drag in as many shots as you like, and change the order in which they appear by simply dragging them backward or forward on the storyboard.

369 Step 7: Add a transition

If you don't want a straight cut between your shots, you can easily add a different transition. Choose Video Transitions from the drop-down list above the Collections window, and you're offered a massive array of transition effects.

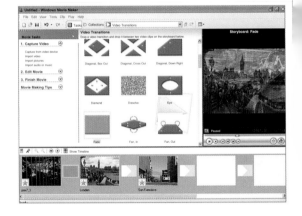

370 Step 8: Adding a fade

By far the most useful is the Fade. Simply drag it to the small box between two of your shots, and when you play back the production, the fade will be in place.

371 Step 9: Trim your edits

We now want to tighten up our edits a little, and that's difficult with the Storyboard view. Click the Show Timeline button just above the storyboard, and MovieMaker switches to a Timeline view.

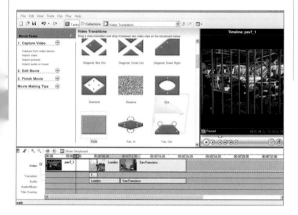

372 Step 10: Shorten a clip in timeline view

Here, you can trim clips by simply placing your cursor between two shots, and clicking and dragging. The monitor shows the frame that's being moved, so you can easily find the point at which you want to cut in or out.

373 Step 11: Special effects

MovieMaker comes with a range of effects—familiarize yourself with them by playing and experimenting with a copy of some footage.

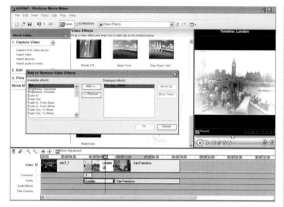

374 Step 12: Select an effect

Adding effects is simple. Just select Video Effects from the drop-down menu above the Collections window, choose an effect, and drag it onto a clip.

375 Step 13: Changing an effect

If you don't like what you see, right-click on the clip, choose Video Effects, and you can remove it again.

376 Step 14: Adding titles

In order to add titles, captions, or credits, simply pick Titles and Credits from the Tools menu.

377 Step 15: Choosing a title

A wizard appears allowing you to add basic titles.

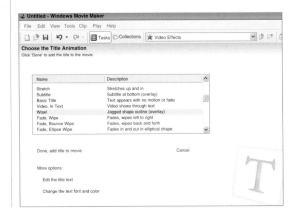

378 Step 16: Adding music

To add music (or other sound effects) just select Import Audio or Music from the menu to the left of the screen.

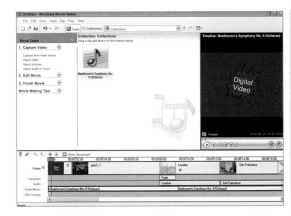

379 Step 17: Selecting audio clips

Now locate any audio clips you have on your hard drive (these can often have a suffix such as MP3, AIFF, Windows Media, or AAC).

380 Step 18: Insert audio clip

These audio files then appear in the Collections window, and can be dragged onto the audio track (the second track from the bottom of the timeline).

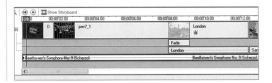

381 Step 19: Complete your video

When you're ready to produce your finished video, MovieMaker offers a number of options under the Finish Movie menu on the left of the screen.

382 Step 20: Choose a format

You can create an email, a CD, a Web page, or a DV tape. Each selection has an easy-to-follow wizard to lead you through the process.

APPLE FINAL CUT PRO/ PRO EXPRESS: PROJECT 1

Apple's iMovie fills the "entry level" role, and then there is Final Cut Pro at the more professional end. This is aimed at editors who demand more effects and more manual control of the edit process. Final Cut Express is the stepping-stone between the two, being a cut-down version of its professional sibling with fewer features but the same basic engine and working methodology.

383 Step 1: Starting a project

Set the Final Cut project for DV use (the US uses NTSC; the UK PAL). Open the Final Cut HD menu and select Easy Setup. Now select DV plus your regional technology (NTSC, PAL, etc) from the dropdown menu.

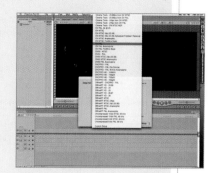

384 Step 2: Capture video 1

Before editing footage, you'll need to capture it to your Mac's hard drive. Select the File menu and click on Log and Capture. This brings up the Log and Capture Control window.

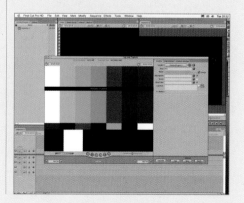

385 Step 3: Capture video 2

By using the transport controls you can view your footage to select an appropriate section to capture. The wheel to the left of the transport controls advances the footage a frame at a time for perfect capture.

386 Step 4: Capture video 3

Having decided what you want to capture, use the slider on the right-hand side to scroll back the footage five seconds before the point you wish to capture. Now press Play and then Capture Now.

387 Step 5: Stop capture

Hit the escape button on your keyboard to stop capturing.

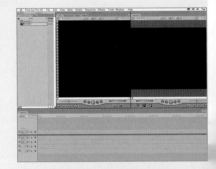

388 Step 6: Name your clip

Now go to the Browser window and select the clip. Click on the name and label it so that you can recognize and locate it easily later. Repeat steps four and five when capturing your clips.

389 Step 7: Place clip on timeline

Drag the clip onto the Canvas window and release it onto the insert pane that appears. This transfers the clip to the timeline at the bottom of the screen. When adding additional clips, be sure to position the playhead where you want the clip to start.

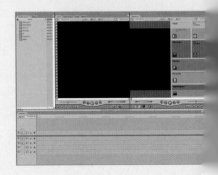

390 Step 8: Trim the clips 1

In order to trim the clip to the required length, you will need to position the playhead where you want the in-point. Select the Blade tool and click that point on the timeline. Repeat the same process for the out-point.

391 Step 9: Trim the clips 2

Select the Arrow tool and highlight any footage that is no longer required. Press the backspace button on the keyboard to delete this footage.

392 Step 10: Trim the clips 3

Add all other clips to the timeline and trim as required. Repeat steps six, seven, and eight to do this. The gaps that you can see between the clips are where we have trimmed them.

393 Step 11: Trim the clips 4

Close the gaps between clips. Position the playhead at the end of the clip. Select the Sequence menu and scroll down to Close Gap. Clicking on this command closes the gaps. Repeat until all gaps are closed.

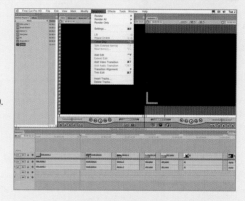

394 Step 12: Adding a transition

In order to create a transition between two clips, place the playhead at the cut-point and click. This highlights the cut-point.

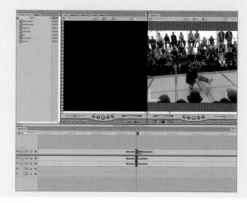

395 Step 13: Adding a dissolve transition

Select the Effects menu at the top of the screen, scroll down to Default-Cross Dissolve and click. This inserts a simple cross dissolve effect.

397 Step 15: Adding a title or caption

Select the Browser window and click on the Effects tab. Open the Video Generators folder and open the Text folder within this. Drag the required effect onto the Viewer window.

396 Step 14: Altering a dissolve

The speed or length of time that the cross dissolve lasts can be adjusted by clicking and holding on either end of the dissolve and dragging to the required length.

398 Step 16: Adding text 1

Select the Controls tab at the top of the Viewer window and type your text into the Text box. Here you can select fonts, point size, and color.

399 Step 17: Adding text 2

Click on the Video tab at the top of the Viewer window. Place the playhead at the start of the clip you want the type to appear over. Now click the center of the Viewer window and drag to the Canvas window, dropping it onto Superimpose.

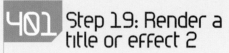

400 Step 18: Render a title or effect 1

The type effect appears on the timeline as a new video layer. You will notice a red bar above it in the Sequence window. This means it needs to be rendered.

401 Step 19: Render a title or effect 2

To render a title or effect, highlight the clip, select the Sequence menu and scroll down to Render Selection. Now click on Both.

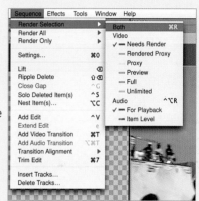

402 Step 20: Output options

Having added as many titles and transitions as required, it is now time to export the finished project back to your camcorder, burn it to disk, or get it ready for emailing! Select the File menu and scroll down to the appropriate option.

APPLE FINAL CUT PRO: PROJECT 2

Final Cut Pro (FCP) is rich and varied, so we've come up with a more advanced project for you to try. In this example, we show you how to edit footage with a professional approach. Before you even start the Mac, take time to pick out the footage you wish to use and, as a professional would, log the relevant start and end points using the timecode on your camcorder.

403 Step 1: Optimizing the screen

FCP has a default setting for the screen layout upon start-up. However, there are a number of different ways of organizing the screen. Here we've opted for larger Viewer Panels to make reviewing footage easier.

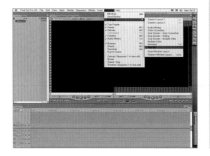

404 Step 2: Determining aspect ratio

Default aspect ratio is 4:3, so if you have shot footage in 16:9, you will need to make the necessary adjustments before capturing. Go to the Sequence Menu at the top of the screen, scroll down to settings, and then check the anamorphic 16:9 box that appears.

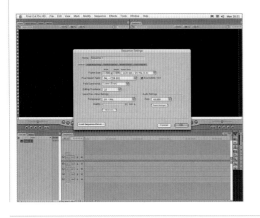

405 Step 3: Open, log, and capture

To open, log, and capture your clips, use a short cut. The Apple key and 8 brings up the Log and Capture window. It is vital to ensure that your camcorder is connected before doing this. You are now ready to input footage.

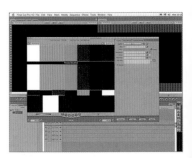

406 Step 4: Creating bins

Bins are folders for your captured footage, providing a logical way for easy retrieval. Clicking on the New Bin icon in the Log and Capture window makes a new folder appear in the Browser window.

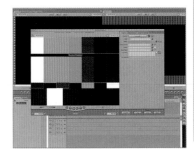

407 Step 5: Setting in and outpoints

Using the timecode of a piece of footage is the most efficient way to capture it. Enter the start point timecode in the left-hand panel, and the end point in the right-hand one.

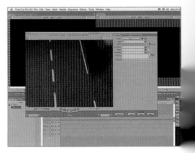

408 Step 6: Naming clips

The logging tab in the Log and Capture window allows you to enter details about the clip such as a description, scene, etc.

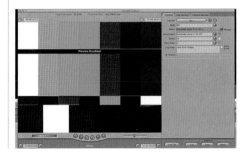

409 Step 7: Logging clips

Having entered those details, we now click the Log Clip button located in the lower-right corner of the Log and Capture window. The clip now appears in the bin that we created earlier.

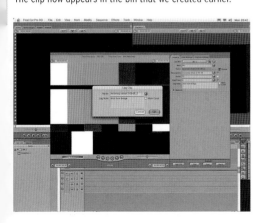

410 Step 8: Batch capture

It is now that the advantage of noting the timecodes becomes clear. Instead of having to go through and individually capture each clip, all clips can be captured by simply pressing the Batch button at the bottom of the Log and Capture.

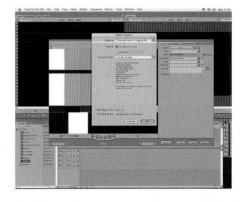

411 Step 9: Importing audio

To import music or a sound effect, go to the File Menu, scroll down to import files and then navigate to your desired audio file.

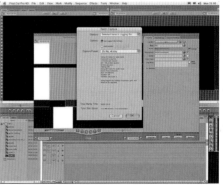

412 Step 10: Importing a QuickTime file

If you have prepared special effects using separate software and have saved them as a QuickTime file, they can be imported. Be sure the file has the same screen size and compression settings as your Final Cut project. Select the File menu, scroll down to Import and then navigate to your desired clip.

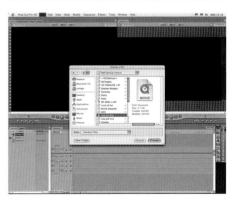

413 Step 11: Importing stills

Select the File menu, scroll down to Import and choose the desired image. The TIFF format is FCP's preferred choice.

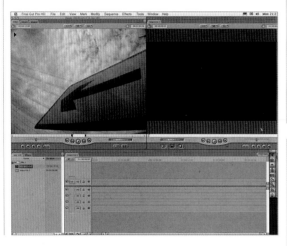

414 Step 12: Placing footage on the timeline

There's a number of different ways to place footage on the timeline. These options appear when you click and drag a clip onto the Canvas window. Insert drops the clip on the playhead, splitting any clips it is placed on top of. As the name suggests, Overwrite overwrites from where the playhead is set.

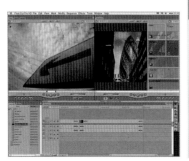

415 Step 13: Fit to Fill

It is possible to timestretch a clip either up or down so that it will fit into a required gap in your sequence. This is carried out using the Fit to Fill function in the Canvas window.

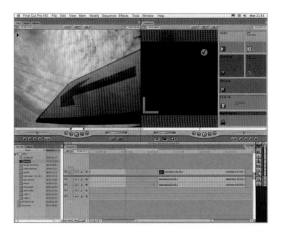

416 Step 14: Video and audio linking

Captured clips come with video and audio tracks linked together. If you wish to replace the audio, you need to unlink the two. Click on the Link Selection button to do this.

417 Step 15: Audio controls

Drag your audio track to the timeline, positioning the playhead at the in-point. To fade it out, use the Blade tool to select where the fade starts and drag the remainder of the audio track into the Viewer window.

418 Step 16: Audio controls

This provides a visual soundwave of the clip, with the pink line representing the volume. Place keyframes at the in and outpoint of the clip. Grabbing and dragging the pink line down at the outpoint ensures a gradual fade.

419 Step 17: Zooming in on a still

Move your still from the timeline onto the Viewer window. Click the Motion tab. Move the playhead to the start of the clip on the Sequence Timeline. Set the scale at which the zoom starts and insert a Keyframe. Place the Playhead at the end of the clip, select the scale at which the zoom ends, and insert another Keyframe.

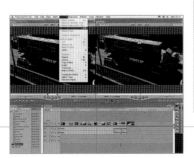

420 Step 18: Creating an effect

Select the required clip, drag and drop it into the Viewer window, select the Effects tab in the browser and click on the Video Filters folder. Now choose the desired effect and drag and drop it onto the viewer window.

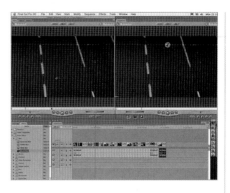

421 Step 19: Rendering your project

To render, select all your clips by pressing the Apple key and A, select the Sequence Menu at the top of the screen, and scroll down to Render All, and click on Both.

422 Step 20: Previewing footage

Position the playhead at the start of the project and press the space bar. The Canvas window can be stretched to fill the screen for a better view.

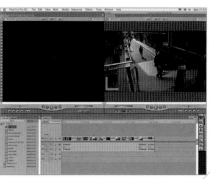

423 What can it do?

Premiere Pro offers significant advantages over more entry-level editors, such as multiple video and audio tracks that allow you to layer many files on top of each other, real-time previews that speed up your work by letting you see special effects and transitions almost instantly, and a much wider array of cuts and customization for effects.

425 ADOBE PREMIERE PRO

Adobe's Premiere Pro is built for the very latest capabilities of the Windows environment. Its cut-down sibling Premiere Elements is Adobe's equivalent to Apple's Final Cut Express. Although some people have talked about Final Cut Pro being a superior package, Premiere Pro has some powerful features that make it a good choice for the aspiring pro.

424 Media window

The Media Window of Premiere Pro can display the clips or audio files stored in the program's bins, letting you check a clip before importing it to the monitor or timeline.

426 Timeline

Unlike more basic programs, Premiere's timeline allows you to create as many video and audio tracks as you want, so you can pile layer upon layer, or carry out fancy transparency effects that allow one track to be seen through another.

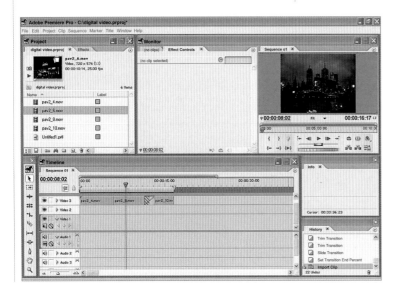

427 History palette

The history palette keeps track of all the cuts, effects, and other changes you've made to your project, so that mistakes can be more easily rectified simply by stepping backwards through your actions.

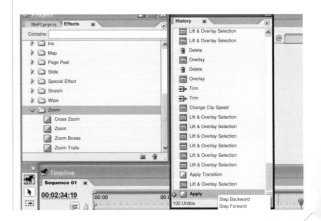

428 Window tabs

Tabbed editors allow you to change the tools on display according to the task you're working on. This is handy with advanced editors, as the sheer volume of extra controls would make the interface extremely cluttered and confusing.

429 Navigator

Because the timeline offers you the opportunity to create such complicated projects, Premiere provides a navigator which represents the contents of the timeline in the form of a small map. Clicking a point on the navigator takes you to the same point on the timeline.

430 Preparing to capture

Before you can capture footage from your camcorder into Premiere, you need to set up your capture preferences. In the File menu, click Preferences, then Scratch Disks and Device Control, then click Enable Device Control.

431 Capturing video from a camcorder

By pressing F5 on your keyboard you can open Premiere's capture window. Click the play button at the bottom to begin scrolling through your tape, and hit the record button at the top of the capture window to import the footage on screen.

432 Batch-capturing video

If you have lots of shots scattered around a tape, it's easier to import using batch capture. Tick the box marked Auto-Record then use the controls to fast forward through your tape and hit the Log In/Out button at the beginning and end of each shot you want. This will compile a list of all the shots you want, which Premiere will then capture from the tape automatically.

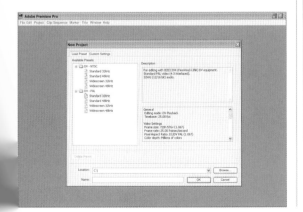

433 Importing multiple files

If there are lots of files you want, you can import them in one go by holding down the CTRL key on your keyboard and clicking them one after the other.

434 Adding clips to the timeline

Hold down the CTRL key and click on the first two shots for your film in the order you want them to appear, then drag them down to the timeline and drop them at the far right of the track marked video one.

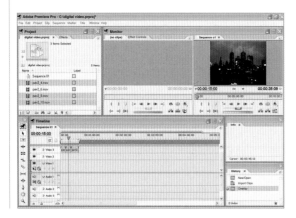

435 Zoom

The timeline will grow each time you add clips, making it hard to see everything at once. Click on the slider at the bottom of the timeline and drag it until the timeline has scaled down enough for you to see where the two clips join.

436 Trim your clip

Click on the end of the first clip and drag it to the right to shorten it. If you look at the right-hand monitor window it will show you the frame you're on. When the frame in the window is the frame you want the clip to end on, release the mouse button. You can drag either end of either clip in this fashion, until they all start and end where you want them to.

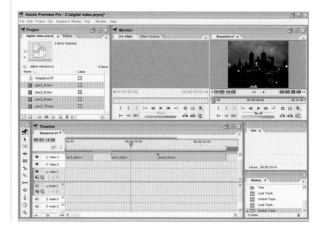

437 Fine-tune the cut

Once you've trimmed the clips, you'll probably find that gaps have appeared in the timeline. To close these, right-click on the gap and select ripple delete. Ripple edits are cuts with effects that ripple outward from the cut and affect the rest of the timeline. By selecting ripple delete, Premiere knows that it needs to move the other clips up to fill the gap.

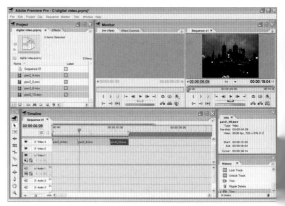

438 Add a cutaway: Step 1

Timeline editing makes it much easier to place cutaways because
you have multiple video tracks. First, click the shot you want to cut
away to and drag it from the media window on to the track marked
video two.

439 Add a cutaway: Step 2

Now click and drag both ends of the new clip inwards until it starts
at the point where your cutaway object is in the monitor window,
and ends about a second later. Click the center of the clip icon on
the timeline and drag it into the position you want it to play at. If,
for example, you want the cutaway to occur one minute into the
footage on video track one, then drag the icon on video track two
until it sits above the one-minute mark on video track one. When
you hit play, the content of track two will be played until the
playhead reaches the one-minute mark and encounters the
footage on track two, which it will cut away to.

440 Opening the effects interface

The tabs in Premiere's interface make it easier to organize all the
different files in the program. If you click the tab marked Effects at
the top of the media window, the screen layout will change to show
a list of all the effects filters available. Click the folder marked
Video Transitions, then choose a transition that you want to use
and drag it onto the timeline between your two clips.

441 Timing a transition

The transition icon that now sits between your clips represents the
effect you've applied. Double-click it to bring up the Effect Controls
window. Type in the number of seconds you want the transition to
take in the box marked duration.

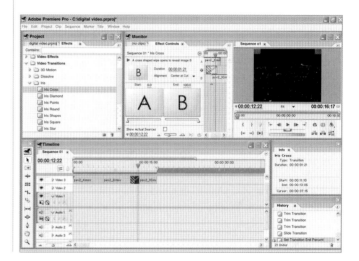

442 Adjusting the transition

By adjusting the two sliders beneath the boxes marked A and B,
you can adjust how much of the transition's duration occurs in the
first clip, and how much in the second. If, for example, you want the
fade to start right at the very end of the first clip and last half way
into the second, drag the slider under box A almost all the way to
the right, and the slider under box B to the middle.

443 Opening the title tool

Premiere Pro's titling tool is opened by clicking on the File menu and selecting first New, then Title from the menus that appear.

444 Draw a text box

The black screen in the middle of the title tool represents your video, with the lines acting as guides for safe areas of the screen where your title won't be cut off. By clicking and dragging in this area you can draw a box for your title to go in. Wherever you place the box is where your text will appear over your video. Create a box and type your title into it.

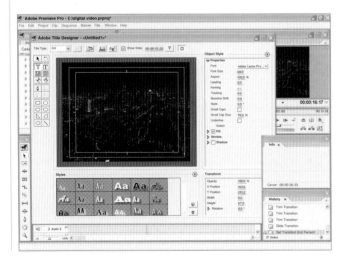

445 Styling your text

The boxes at the bottom of the screen show the various text styles you can choose, while the parameters at the left can be used to adjust everything from how close together the letters are, whether they cast a shadow on the video beneath them, and even how opaque they are. Your title doesn't become final until you save it, so you can play around with these settings as much as you like.

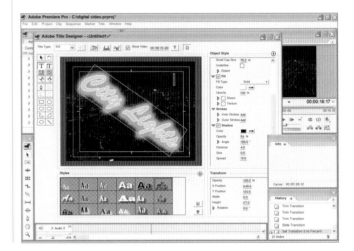

446 Adding titles to the timeline

Once your title looks the way you want it to, click the File menu and save the title, then click the red X to close the title tool and return to the main Premiere interface. After a few seconds, the title will appear in the media window, where it can be moved to the timeline, trimmed, and manipulated just like a video clip.

447 Opening the title shortcuts menu

Drag your title from the media window onto video track two so it sits above your main video clip. Click the title's icon on the timeline to select it, then right-click it to open the shortcut menu.

448 Displaying your title over video

In the shortcut menu, scroll down to Video Options and click Transparency. A settings box will appear with a drop-down menu marked key type. Click this menu and select Alpha Channel. Then click OK.

449 Adjusting a title transparency

An alpha channel is a track of video information that relates the transparency of one clip to the opacity of another, allowing you to see one clip or title over another by making part of the background transparent. Click the arrow next to Video Two at the right of the timeline to display the alpha channel. Click and drag the red line to rubberband the transparency, fading it up and down in order to fade your title in and out of the video beneath it.

450 Saving or exporting

You can save your project by selecting Save As in the File menu, to preserve it for further changes later on. A nice feature in Premiere, however, is an instant export to DVD feature that allows you to make a basic DVD very easily. In the File menu, select Export, then Export to DVD. When the dialog box appears, select the option marked Auto-Play then hit record.

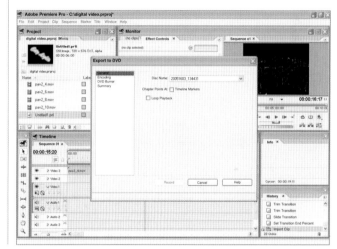

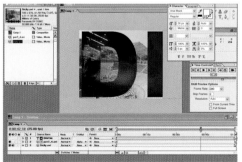

Video Output

Sharing Your Video

Finally we get to the best bit, the culmination of all your work–sharing your video with an audience, be it family, friends, or strangers on the other side of the world. In this section we'll give you a few pointers about how your video should be prepared, and tell you how to use the most common methods of distribution.

451 Things to think about

Before you begin exporting your video, it's important to work out a few things, most notably who is your audience and where are they? There are certain guidelines for submitting video to producers or TV companies that don't apply to family and friends, and of course, there are different TV systems in operation around the world that need to be taken into account.

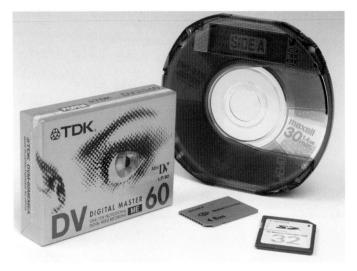

452 At any rate

NTSC is the television system in use in the US and Japan. It has a horizontal resolution of 525 lines, and a frame rate of 30 frames per second.

453 Be a PAL

In the UK, Australia, and most of Europe, televisions and VCRs use the Phase Alternating Line system, in which 625 lines of horizontal resolution are displayed, but at a slower rate of 25 frames per second.

454 SECAM

Sequential Couleur Avec Memoire is the television system used in France. A version of it known as MESECAM is also used in the Middle East. If you're planning to send tape or DVD to these countries, you need to adjust the preferences setting in your NLE system to the correct television standard in order to make the finished result compatible.

455 Give it some room

Another effect of the differing television standards around the world is that the safe area of the screen changes. The safe area is the part in which any titles, captions, or action will definitely be shown. Anything outside the safe area runs the risk of being cropped out by the TV. If you're authoring a DVD, go into preferences and select Show Safe Area, then set it to whichever standard is relevant. This will place guidelines on the screen, inside which menu buttons and suchlike can be safely placed.

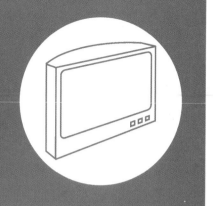

456 Behind bars

Color bars are like the professional version of a TV test card. If you're sending your video to a producer or commissioning agent, it's traditional to add color bars to the start of the sequence so that they can adjust their monitor. This is because quality standards are higher for TV or corporate work, and they'll want to see whether your work is good enough at its best. Color bars can be added by your editing software at the export stage. Traditionally, you have color bars on screen for 59 seconds, with your video starting at the one-minute mark.

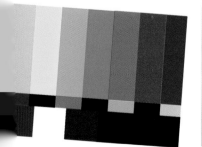

EXPORTING VIDEO TO DV TAPE

As we've seen in the earlier chapters on editing, all non-linear editing programs allow you to export the final cut of your video back to tape. Tape may seem old hat in these days of DVD and Internet video but, as widespread formats, DV or VHS tape offer almost everyone an easy way to watch your video.

457 Rendering your project

Most NLE systems offer you a real time preview of effects and transitions so that you can see what you're working on, but these previews won't transfer to tape. In order to get all the wipes, effects, and titles in your project onto tape, you have to render them. With your project on the timeline, click the Render All option and the computer will finalize all the effects ready for export.

458 Save to hard drive

Some older NLE systems won't allow you to export directly from their timeline and insist you save your edit as a video file prior to export. This is as easy as saving a word processor document—simply select Save Project As, pick a destination on your hard drive, and hit OK.

459 Crystal clear

Crystal Blacking is used to smooth the progress of transferring video from computer to tape by laying down a continuous data stream on the tape that can be followed by the export process. Put your final tape into the camcorder, put the lens cap on, and hit record until the tape runs out. The tape is now Blacked and ready to receive your video.

460 Choose a format and standard

Modern NLE systems provide all sorts of options for tape formats and video standards, and it's important to pick the right one. If you're exporting to DV, select DV not DV cam. If your tape is going to be sent overseas, find out what standard is used at the tape's destination and select it as your export option.

461 Set a pre roll

Pre roll is the amount of time the tape is rolling for before recording starts. Pre roll allows the tape transport mechanism to get up to normal speed and past the blank leader tape so that the start of your video isn't distorted or cut off. In the box for pre roll select at least eight seconds delay prior to recording.

462 Select an abort level

If you're using an older, slower computer, or are exporting from a slow hard drive (one that spins at around 5,200 RPM or slower) there is the possibility that it won't be able to keep up with the export process and will drop frames. This means losing video on the way to the tape. Too many dropped frames will be noticeable on your video, so the computer offers you the option to abort the transfer after a certain number of frames have been dropped. Any more than one or two dropped frames suggests a problem that needs fixing, so set the abort number quite low, or even at just one.

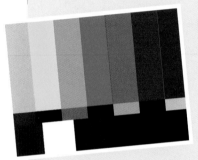

463 Add color bars

In your export settings box, click the checkbox marked color bars. Then, in the pane that appears, type in 59 seconds. You can skip this for most exports, but if your video is going to a producer or commissioning editor, color bars will usually be required.

464 Export

Having set the export options, hit the export button and the computer will take control of your camcorder and begin transferring the video. This process will take fractionally longer than the duration of your video.

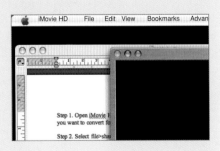

EXPORTING FROM DV TO VHS

465 Old-fashioned formats

VHS is an even more widespread format than DV, and even though it has much lower picture quality it does offer your film a very big audience. Transferring DV to VHS is a simple process. First, follow the process just detailed to get your video onto a DV tape in your camcorder.

466 Connect your camcorder and VCR

You can connect your camcorder to your VCR in three ways. The most common method is to use the AV connection cable that comes with your camcorder, this is the cable with the 3.5mm jack at one end and the red, white (audio), and yellow (video) connectors at the other. These connectors can be plugged into the correspondingly colored socket on the back of your VCR, or into a Scart adaptor (also supplied with your camcorder) which is then plugged into the Scart socket on your VCR. This is the most commonly used connection as all VCRs have AV inputs and most have a 21-pin Scart socket.

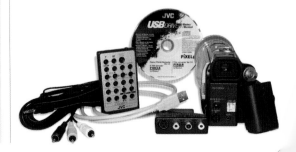

467 S-Video

For higher quality you can hook your camcorder's S-Video output to the VCR's S-Video input. S-Video processes color and brightness (chrominance and luminance) signals separately for better quality but isn't available on all camcorders and VCRs.

468 Moving with the times

In an attempt to stave off obsolescence, some VCRs now feature a DV input and can convert an incoming DV signal for recording to analog VHS tape. This is the best option of all, if your VCR is capable of it.

469 Hit it

Once your camcorder is connected to your VCR by one of the methods above, dubbing across is as easy as recording from the television. Simply press play on your camcorder and record on your VCR. Unlike DV tapes, there is no point in blacking a VHS tape as it won't hold a timecode.

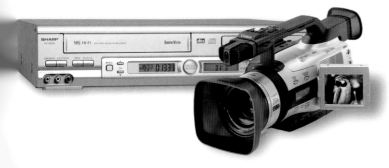

MAKE A VCD OR DVD

470 What's an MPEG?

MPEG stands for Motion Picture Experts Group, and put simply it's a type of compression. That is, all the masses of data that make up a video is squashed down to a size that fits onto a disk, hopefully with as little loss of quality as possible. DVDs use a version called MPEG2. VCDs use a lower quality called MPEG or MPEG1. There's even a sort of middle ground called MPEG4 which is good for making videos that can be posted on Web sites or in emails.

471 How does it work?

All video-editing programs have in them a codec (compressor/decompressor). When you choose MPEG or MPEG2 in your export settings box the codec takes every frame of video and identifies what has changed between frames. If you have a sequence with a tree and roadside in the foreground, and a car moving past in the background, the codec knows that it doesn't need to save all the information that relates to the foreground, just the stuff that relates to the car in the background. So, the more movemement there is, the harder the codec has to work.

472 What is a bitrate?

Your codec is taking your video and squashing it down to a manageable size by ignoring anything that doesn't change from frame to frame. However, when there's a lot of movement, that means a lot of changes, so the codec has less to discard and more to keep. That's where bitrates come in. The bitrate is the amount of information contained in a second of video. If you set a high bitrate, then your video quality will be higher, as the codec will store more information about the changes and keep track of them better, but this will mean that the file size will be larger as more information is retained. That's the game with compression: balancing the quality of the video against the capacity of the disk.

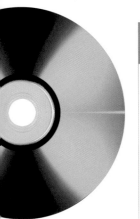

473 VCD and SVCD

VCD (Video Compact Disk) and its flashier big brother SVCD (SuperVCD) are similar to DVD in as much as they consist of video files compressed into MPEG and burnt onto a disk. The major difference is that they are written to CD rather than DVD, resulting in much heavier compression in order to fit onto the lower-capacity disks. For this, they use MPEG rather than MPEG2.

474 Quality and compatibility

VCDs are of similar picture quality to VHS but have the advantage of being cheaper to produce, playable in computers and many DVD players, and easier to mail to far-off people. Another advantage is that VCDs can be produced using a CD Burner and either CD creation or NLE software, whereas DVDs require you to splash out on more expensive DVD-creation software and hardware. However, it's worth noting that not all DVD players can handle VCD. Strangely, it's usually the cheaper players that are sold in markets all around the world that are designed with broad compatibility in mind, so if you want to play VCDs it's usually a good idea to buy a cheap and cheerful DVD player.

475 Pick a program

Your options for creating VCDs are very broad indeed. If you are a Windows-user you'll find that almost every NLE program has a "create VCD" option in the export menu. If you use Apple editing software you'll find that only DVD creation is supported. However, products such as Roxio's Toast are inexpensive and offer a VCD option. You can even search the Web for VCD Creation Freeware and find plenty of totally free programs for compressing and burning video files from your hard drive to VCD. VCD creation involves compressing the video very carefully, due to the massive reduction in data rate. There is little margin for error, which actually makes things easier for beginners, as your VCD creation template will, of necessity, be forced to do all the work rather than leaving it in your hands. VCD creation therefore tends to be a one-step process.

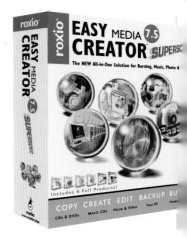

476 Make a DVD

Pretty much the star of the show these days, DVD is the most successful home entertainment technology ever, in terms of the speed of its market penetration. Just about everyone now has a DVD player, meaning that DVD is an excellent way to share your videos. The exact terms used by the various authoring programs vary, but the procedure for making a DVD remains the same.

477 DVD, Blu-Ray, HD-DVD

DVD-R and DVD+R are two long-established, competing versions of the same format, but both will play in a standard home player. Rewriteable versions (DVD-RW and DVD+RW) are also available. Two emerging formats are Blu-Ray and HD-DVD. Both offer vastly superior, multi-gigabyte storage capacities, but hardware for each format is not yet compatible with the other, so choose extremely carefully. Both new formats require special players/recorders, as data is written using blue lasers rather than the standard red.

478 The write tools for the job

There are two methods for creating your own DVDs from a DV tape, the first is a FireWire-equipped DVD recorder, the second is a DVD burner in your computer.

479 The easy way

The easiest method is to use a DVD recorder with a FireWire input. Like VCRs, DVD recorders are essentially DVD players that can also be used to record from TV. If, however, you get one equipped with a FireWire port, you can simply plug in your camcorder and hit record just like you would with VHS. This is the easiest method of putting your work on DVD, but it lacks the flexibility and creative control provided by a burner.

480 Feel the burn

Using a burner built into your computer is the best way of creating a DVD similar to the ones you buy in the shops. You get to have a moving menu background, buttons, multiple scenes, even surround sound audio, and subtitles if you have an advanced authoring program. To create a DVD this way, all you need is a burner built into your computer, which is commonplace these days, and an authoring package that will let you design the menus and encode the video.

481 Author, author!

Authoring is the term used for creating a playable MPEG of your video and designing a menu that will work with it. Authoring packages range from the free ones that come installed on your computer, such as Apple's iDVD and Sony's ClickToDVD, through to inexpensive beginners' programs that guide you through the process step by step, such as Ulead's DVD Workshop, all the way up to the sort of programs that will let you create surround sound, manage multiple angles, and create subtitles and special features, such as Apple's DVD Studio Pro or Adobe Encore.

482 A new chapter

Chapter points are a common feature on shop-bought DVDs and can also be a feature on your homemade ones. We mention them first because all of the editing packages we walked you through in the last section allow you to create chapter markers in your video before you even open it with your authoring program. Simply play through the timeline, stop the playhead where you want a chapter point to be, then hit the add chapter marker in the Markers menu.

483 To put it another way

You can also add chapter markers within your authoring program. Your first step is to click the File menu and select Import or Get Video, which will bring your DV footage from your hard drive into the authoring program. Then you can drag the footage into the preview window, play it, and hit the space bar to mark chapter points.

484 What's on the menu?

Next you have to choose a menu background. All DVD authoring programs come with a selection of themed templates that you can use as the background onto which you place all your buttons. These can be customized by changing the text to something relevant, and by adding pictures and sometimes moving video loops.

485 Loop length

If your authoring program supports looped videos then you'll be able to drag a piece of video from the browser that contains all your files, and drop it onto the menu, where it will play in a repeating loop. This makes your menu more interesting, but be careful to choose the right piece of video. Too long and it will waste disk space, too short and you'll be subjecting your audience to a tortuous repetition. About 30 seconds is a good length for a loop.

486 Add buttons

Your authoring program will have provided some ready-made buttons on the template, and will have a button marked Add Button which you can click to create more controls on your menu. Once your buttons are on the menu background, you add video to them simply by clicking on the relevant video file in the browser and dragging onto the correct button.

487 Margin of error

Hopefully, your authoring program will have safe area guides that will show you which part of your menus will be safely displayed on any TV set. If it doesn't, a simple rule of thumb is to imagine a danger area of 10% around the edge of the screen like a border—this is the area where buttons or graphics risk being cropped. Try not to place anything in it.

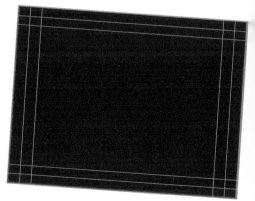

488 Customize your buttons

Now that your buttons are placed and have video attached, you can customize them. By double-clicking the text that says Button1 you can highlight it and type a more descriptive title. By double-clicking the button itself, you'll be presented with a slider that will allow you to skim through the video attached to the button until you find a fitting frame of video to be displayed in the button.

489 Keep it simple

You don't want your audience getting lost in the branches of your menu when all they want is to watch your video. For this reason, it's best to keep your main menu screen as simple as possible. One button marked play movie and another that links to a second menu page for special features and chapter selection is ideal.

490 Preview mode

When you think your menu is finished, hit the preview button. This brings up an imitation DVD remote control with all the buttons you'd find on the real thing. Use this to navigate around your disk in the same way your audience would. Do all the buttons work? Do they all link to something? Does the menu structure make sense? If you can say yes to all these questions, you're ready to burn the disk.

491 Choose bitrate

We mentioned bitrates earlier, now here's where they come into play. If the video on your disk is very short, you'll probably be able to choose a nice high bitrate of around 7 or 8 MBps. If it's longer you'll need a smaller bitrate to make it fit. You can also use VBR (variable bit rate). This allows the codec to increase the bitrate for complex sections of video, and reduce it for simpler ones, achieving the best balance of quality and compression. An online search for bitrate calculators will provide you with tools for figuring out how high a bitrate your video will allow.

492 Choose a burnspeed

Your burner is doing just that, burning marks into your disk. The laser that reads the disk is reading the differences between the way it reflects from burnt and unburnt patches. For this reason, precision is very important. When you come to burn the disk you'll be offered speeds such as 2x, 4x, 16x, etc. These control how fast the burning laser moves around the disk. Unless you're really pushed for time, it's better to use a slower speed, as this will make the burns more precise, as well as saving wear and tear on the mechanical parts that move the laser head around.

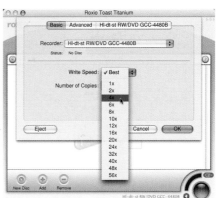

493 Going online

Putting your video online is the most popular way of making sure anyone can see it, although it does involve drastically reducing the image size and quality. But that's a small price to pay for making your video accessible to the whole world. You can prepare video for the Web from inside your editing software, and host it on your own Web site, or a specialist site such as Google's Video Blog, Mydeo.com, or Atomfilms.com.

495 Realplayer

Realplayer is platform-independent and has to be downloaded rather than coming supplied with your computer. It benefits from regular upgrades, but be warned, it can occasionally cause problems on older machines, and the regular upgrades that keep it cutting edge also mean that older versions of the player frequently become obsolete.

496 Windows Media Player

Thanks to the near ubiquity of Windows-based computers, Windows Media files are the ones most likely to be compatible with the broadest audience possible.

494 Quicktime

There are three main tools for creating and playing Web and email video: Quicktime, Realplayer, and Windows Media. In the export options box of your video-editing software you'll be presented with choices for one, two, or all three, depending on the program you use. Quicktime is Apple's media player, although, like all three, there are versions available for all computer platforms. The in-built Quicktime codec, H.264, is specifically designed with Web video in mind, although all three players are primarily used for Web video, so are all suitable for the purpose.

497 Screen size

Having chosen what type of file to make, you need to choose a screen size. Reducing the screen size helps make the file size smaller. With broadband connections being commonplace these days, you don't need to shrink the picture down to postage-stamp size, but a reasonable size reduction will cater for both broadband and dial-up users. We'd suggest selecting 320 x 240 in the options list. Alternatively, you could make multiple versions in order to cater for all connection types.

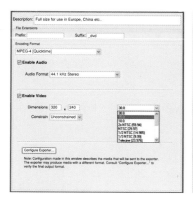

498 Frame rate

By reducing the frame rate you massively decrease the number of individual images the codec needs to compress, although you simultaneously make the video jumpier, as the "persistence of vision" effect upon which video works is decreased. A good middle ground is about 15Fps. This will be noticeably less smooth than ordinary video, but not disruptively so.

499 Audio

Sorry to say it, but even though you can't see sound, it still takes up space in your video file. Unless it's vital that you have stereo audio, we'd suggest you select mono audio in the encode settings box, as this will save on file size without wrecking the sound.

500 Encode

Having chosen all your encode preferences, you can hit the save button and the codec will begin creating the video to your specifications. This may take a while depending on the length of your video, but by the time you're finished you'll have what this whole book has been leading up to–a great video that can be shared with anyone, anywhere in the world.

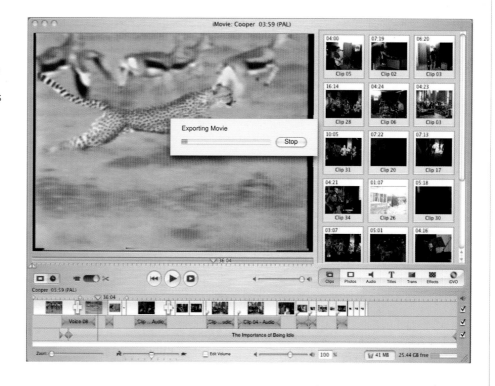

Technical Terms
The technical terms, abbreviations, and digital jargon used in the text are summarized below for your further reference and information.

A-D convertor
A device attached to a computer and an analog camcorder or VCR which converts analog information from the tape into digital information that can be used by the computer.

Anamorphic lens
A lens similar to a wideangle lens except it only enhances the width and not the height, creating a widescreen aspect ratio.

Aperture
The opening created by the iris between the lens and CCD. The wider the iris, the larger the aperture and the more light reaches the CCD.

Aspect ratio
The width-to-height ratio of the screen or the image upon it.

Assemble editing
The linear editing process of cutting together a film by copying scenes, one-by-one, from tape to tape.

Audio dub
Some camcorders allow you to leave an audio track free so that you can dub extra audio onto your footage later without disturbing the original sound.

BLC (Backlight Compensation)
A function that boosts the gain of subjects lit from the rear to avoid an unwanted silhouette effect.

Batch capture
The process of telling an NLE system the specific start and end points of several pieces of footage that you want imported from your camcorder. Batch capture allows you to spend time on other jobs while your computer takes control of your camcorder and imports the footage that you have asked for.

Bit
The smallest piece of digital information. There are eight bits (binary digits) to a byte.

Bluetooth
Named after a Danish king, Bluetooth is a wireless data transfer method that allows compatible devices to communicate with each other. For example, a Bluetooth laptop could use a Bluetooth cellphone to access the Internet.

Blu-Ray (disk)
A new ultra-high-capacity disk format encoded by blue laser rather than red. HD-DVD is a competing format.

Burn
The process of permanently writing information to a recordable disk, such as a CD or DVD.

Byte
A quantity of digital information. There are eight bits to a byte.

Capture card
A board fitted to a computer that allows video to be captured to the hard disk via IEEE1394 (FireWire/i.Link) cable, and sent back to the camcorder after editing.

CCD (Charge Coupled Device)
The imaging chip that registers the light coming through the lens with varying degrees of electrical charge that are used to recreate the picture.

Chromakey
The process of replacing one of the colors in a shot with a still image or a piece of video—similar to a bluescreen shot.

Codec
An abbreviation of compressor/decompressor: a tool for reducing the file size of video by compression. Codecs use algorithms to discard certain data and save only the important changes. These algorithms are later used to reconstitute the image. Codecs can be either hardware or software.

Component
Component video separates the chroma and luminance signals of a video and processes them separately to give sharper and richer images.

Composite
Composite video processes chroma and luminance simultaneously, but at a lesser quality than component.

Compression
The process of making files smaller by discarding unnecessary data, creating a "shorthand" version of the data to be used to reconstitute the picture later.

CPU (Central Processing Unit)
The processing unit of your computer, such as a G5 or Pentium 4. Essentially a microchip with a basic understanding of the words "yes" and "no". By performing millions of calculations per second, the processor does your computer's "thinking".

Device control

The ability to control a camcorder or deck from within a piece of editing software, allowing you to run the camcorder without touching it.

Download

The process of importing a file from a remote location to your own computer.

Driver

Software that makes a particular peripheral device work with your computer. Usually supplied with the device in question, and often also downloadable.

DVD

Digital Versatile (or Video) Disk. A high-capacity disk, on which video or data can be stored. Video is usually stored in the compressed MPEG2 format. Competing types of recordable DVD include +R/RW, -R/RW, and DVD-RAM, which vary in size, capacity, and compatibility. The differences are primarily in the way information is burnt to disk. Emerging formats such as Blu-Ray require dedicated hardware.

Extension

A three-letter suffix that allows you and your computer to distinguish between different types of file. Examples include .MOV (QuickTime), and .JPG (JPEG photo).

EDL (Edit Decision List)

Usually, however not necessarily, a computer-generated list that records the location of all the shots in a project and keeps track of the changes made to them. Helpful in reconstructing a rough cut from higher quality footage.

FireWire

Apple's term for an IEEE1394 cable and its associated devices, used to transfer data at high speed. Newer, faster versions of FireWire are known as FireWire 800 after the higher data-rate.

Flash memory

Memory devices, usually removable, with no moving parts. Data such as small video files, MP3s, digital still photographs, and suchlike can be stored on flash memory on one device and transferred to another. Examples include Compact Flash, Memory Stick, SD Card, and MMC.

Generation loss

The loss of quality associated with each generation away from a master copy. For example, a first-generation copy will be of higher quality than a second, and so on.

Hard disk

The large magnetic disk within a computer upon which programs and files are stored.

HD (High-definition)

A video format of very high quality. Often touted as a potential replacement for film.

Hot-pluggable

The term for devices that can be plugged into a computer and used without the need to restart the computer.

Hot shoe

A powered accessory shoe on a camcorder for mounting lights, microphones, etc, where they can draw power from the main battery or be controlled by the buttons on the camcorder.

Insert editing

A cut that replaces a section of video but leaves the original audio intact. Ideal for reaction shots and cutaways.

JPEG

A standard for compressing still photographic images. Originally named after the Joint Photographic Experts Group.

Jitter

Jarring movement and color errors at the top of a video image caused by poor timing. Very rare in digital video.

Jump cut

A noticeable change in framing or perspective between two edits, causing the subject to appear to "jump" from one position to another. Usually considered a mistake, but often used for dramatic effect.

Keyframe

One of a series of marked frames in a video that allows for complicated effects to be simplified. By marking the state of the effect at certain keyframes, the effects software can be left to figure out what comes in-between.

Key light

The main light used on a subject, influencing the intensity of the rest of the scene's lighting.

Linear editing

The process of assembling a film by copying shots to tape sequentially.

Lux

A measure of ambient light. Daylight is usually around 10,000 lux. Some camcorders can operate at as little as 0 lux.

Macro

A function that allows a camcorder to remain focused on an object extremely close to the lens. Good for shooting small items.

Metadata

Information about a piece of video that isn't the actual sound and vision itself. Includes compression ratios, television standards, etc.

Motion-JPEG

A compression method that applies JPEG-style compression to moving images.

MPEG

A compression standard for moving images, named after the Motion (or Moving) Picture Experts Group. Works by storing critical frames and the differences between them as opposed to the full footage. Variations include MPEG1 (a lower quality compression used in VCDs), MPEG4 (used for email video), and MPEG2 (used on DVDs). The compressed audio format MP3 is derived from MPEG.

Night mode

A method of shooting in low light conditions. Two versions are commonly used. Slow-shutter night modes allow a longer exposure time for the CCD to absorb available light, but in the process expose each frame to more motion in the picture causing jumpy images. Infrared modes work at ordinary shutter speeds so avoid jumpiness, but by absorbing light frequencies not normally visible the images tend to take on a distinctive green cast.

NLE (Non-linear Editing)

The process of using a computer or "one box editor" to construct a video from footage saved to hard disk. Because non-linear editing doesn't involve working with the original material it is non-destructive, allowing you to work in any order you wish before saving the completed project and sending it back to tape or disk.

NTSC (National Television System Committee)

Television system of 525 lines used mainly in the US, Canada, South America, and parts of the Caribbean.

OHCI (Open Host Controller Interface)

An agreed standard that allows different manufacturers to produce compatible equipment, drivers, and software.

PAL (Phase Alternating Line)

A television standard of 625 lines at 25fps used in many parts of the world, including the UK, much of Western Europe, parts of Asia, and Australia.

Patch

A small computer program added to a larger one to remedy defects.

Peripherals

External devices attached to a computer such as printers and scanners.

Pixel (Picture Element)

The smallest element of an image on a monitor or in a digital photo.

Program AE mode

Program AE (autoexposure) is a preset combination of exposure, white balance, and shutter speed settings.

QuickTime

A media player and file format developed by Apple and available for Mac or PC.

RAM (Random Access Memory)

The short-term memory of your computer that holds the information needed to run programs and the information being used by those programs.

Rendering

The process of your computer working out all the changes made to a piece of video by

an effect and applying them. Faster processors render more quickly, and certain capture cards include separate processors for handling rendering.

Secam (Sequential Couleur avec Memoire)

Television system of 625 lines used in France, and in parts of Africa, Eastern Europe, and the Middle East.

Streaming

Streaming media is played as it downloads from the Internet and is simultaneously discarded from RAM, making playback quicker and avoiding hard disk clutter.

Timecode

A code carried that allows for accurate editing and synchronization to the number of hours, minutes, seconds, and frames within the file.

Upload

The process of transferring files from your PC to a remote server.

USB (Universal Serial Bus)

A hot-pluggable standard for connecting peripherals to a PC. The most recent version, USB2.0, can function at speeds of up to 480Mbps.

VCD (Video CD)

An inexpensive, low quality alternative to DVD, comprising of MPEG1 footage stored on an ordinary CD.

Wildtrack

Sound recorded independently from the pictures for later dubbing.

Wipe

Editing term. Visual transition in which one image is replaced by another at a boundary edge moving across the picture.

XLR connector

An input used for audio recording found on higher-end camcorders. Provides significantly better sound quality than ordinary 3.5mm microphone jacks.

3Y/C

Component video comprising separate chroma (C) and luminance (Y) signals.

YUV

Component video comprising of luminance (Y) and two color difference signals (U and V).

Zoom

Zooming changes the distance between the lens and the CCD in order to magnify distant objects at the expense of the foreground.

Index

Acknowledgments

Many thanks to Kevin Nixon, Jake Williams, Henryk Simpson
and Andre Whitbourn, who helped a great deal by lending
their time and experience.
Jamie Ewbank

Thanks to all who helped on the book. In no particular order
a hearty handshake should go to Susannah Donnelly, Nick
Donnelly, and Kevin Nixon for their images; Albert Hull, Alice
Hull, and Miriam Brent for their encouragement, and Jaffa
Cakes for their energy (and only 1g of fat per cake).
Rob Hull

The editors would like to thank Gary Miller for footage from
his movie Tom Cat, and Ed Cooper for the additional grabs.